Riding across the Roof of the World

by

I0130421

Wilfred Skrede

The Long Riders' Guild Press

www.thelongridersguild.com

ISBN: 1-59048-040-6

Across the Roof of the World

TIEN SHAN

TAKLA MAKAN (DESERT)

TURKISTAN

TIBET

INDIA

CHINA

U.S.S.R.

KASHGAR

PAMIRS

AFGHANISTAN

GILGIT

ASIA

AFRICA

EUROPE

Lake Balkhash

Contents

Illustrations

^^^^^^^^^^^^^^^^^^^^^^^^^^^^^^^^^^^^^^

Preface

/\\

IN A WAY it is due to the war that this book came to be
written, but the reader will find in it little of what he usually associates with that.

My attempt to reach the training camp for the Norwegian Air Force at Little Norway in Toronto, Canada,
took me right through Russia, into China where I broke my
back, then through the desert of Takla Makan and across
the Karakorum and the Himalayas to Kashmir and Singapore and New York. If anyone with a decent knowledge
of ethnography and other such high-falutin' subjects had
made that trip with the intention of writing a book about
it, the result would have been darned fine, I am sure. But
I was only just nineteen when I left the workshop in Oslo
where I was apprenticed, and my only intellectual asset
was the boundless curiosity of youth.

I know that I have no very valuable information to give
either about geography or ethnography, but I did see a
number of things I thought were strange and wonderful,
and, with the help of some tattered diaries in which I re-
corded impressions in ungrammatical sentences, I have
tried to write about them. I am not even sure that I have

spelt the names of places correctly, still less the few phrases in foreign tongues.

Here, then, is my account of things as I saw them in all innocence and ignorance: of strange and distant lands, of times when my heart was in my boots and others when life seemed wonderful, of days spent among swarms of weird people, and of lonely nights beneath the stars.

WILFRED SKREDE

Across the Roof of the World

1. From Oslo to Xiptoc

/\\!

A CEILING of light thin cloud lay above the steppe which stretched, naked and desolate, as far as the eye could reach. A dust-laden heat haze surrounded the interminable sand-dunes and the grey mud huts of Xiptoc with a shimmer of luminous brown and grey, and beyond the watch-tower of the frontier guards—the only thing that stood up at all from that flat expanse—lay the Ili plain of East Turkestan, greyish-brown, desolate and dry, unknown and endless.

On that stony plain, just outside Xiptoc, stood four young men, little more than youths, with cigarettes dangling in the corners of their mouths and their hands thrust deep in the pockets of their black riding breeches. Their tall well-polished riding boots gave them all the nice comforting feeling that they were pretty fine fellows.

Just at the spot where the youths were standing, the sand must have been mixed with a little earth for here and there grew a wretched tuft of grass and there were a few red and yellow flowers growing among the stones.

The four stood watching a yellowish-white cloud of sand-dust that was careering hither and thither out on the steppe; then it described a long arc, made straight for the youths and became a detachment of Russian cavalry at full gallop. As the sweating, shining, hairy-hoofed horses thundered past there was a gleam of white teeth in the young brown faces which were bent forward above the horses' necks, grinning in savage barbaric glee at the rush and speed of it all. The four spectators, however, were Norwegians. They were on their way to Little Norway in Canada, and as it had not been so long since they had seen tanks and motorized infantry in the streets of Oslo they felt justified in sneering and shrugging their shoulders:

'Cavalry, good heavens! In modern warfare!'

Then they sauntered back to their quarters in the ante-room of the Customs House in Xiptoc.

On the trodden earth floor of that little room lay all their worldly belongings: four bulging rucksacks, an equal number of sleeping-bags, a large accordion, two mandolines, two balalaikas, and ten bottles of champagne which had cost them twenty-seven roubles apiece. The instruments were not in tune, and none of the four could play them or even sing so very prettily, thus it was little wonder that when they struck up, the Russian customs officer, who sat cross-legged like a tailor on the floor, should have shuddered as though he were cold. In his own mind he must have been thinking that little in the world was as ghastly and horrible as Norwegian music.

However, they opened a bottle of champagne, filled a tumbler and handed it to the Russian. '*Skål,*' said they. '*Booddte zdarovee,*' said the Russian, and downed the contents of the tumbler in one gulp. Then he reached out for a mandoline, tuned it, and soft notes began stealing out into the room, crooning to the big portraits of Lenin and Stalin on the walls, notes redolent of the mystery of the steppe. It looked for all the world as though Lenin winked an eye and a smile of recognition flickered beneath Stalin's moustache. The four Norwegians fell silent, and while the twilight of an April evening began to fall on Xiptoc they savoured alternately their champagne and the age-old melancholy of the plains of Kazakstan.

But where, you ask, is Xiptoc? And what on earth were four Norwegian youths doing there with a pile of musical instruments and a small cellar of champagne?

As to the first question: Xiptoc is a small village and it lies more or less in the centre of Asia—to be more exact on the frontier between Soviet Russian Kazakstan and the Chinese province of Sinkiang. And the reason why the four Norwegians were sitting in that dusty grey hole in the middle of the steppe, was that the route they had elected to take in order to reach Canada happened to pass through Xiptoc.

Before we go on perhaps it would be best to explain things a little, or the reader will not know what it was all about.

In the wintry beginning of 1941 a number of Norwegians arrived in Stockholm on the first leg of their journey to join the Allied Forces. The various reasons for their coming there and the different ways of their going, as well as what they intended to do when they reached their destination, are no concern of ours. Suffice it to say that when Andrew and I left Oslo at the end of January it was in the belief that if we could once get to Stockholm, our Legation there would arrange for our further transport to Canada across Russia, Siberia and Japan.

It was not just as simple as that. Many others were ahead of us, and those with technical qualifications—pilots and mechanics—had priority. There was nothing to be done about it. But the worst was that the Japs had closed their frontiers to our transports and it proved impossible to get people away by another route such as across Russia and Turkey. Gradually we began to see that there was every likelihood of our remaining in Sweden as long as the war should last. It was then also pretty obvious that it would last a good long time.

After thinking things over, I and four others, Andrew, Sverre, Kai and Atle, came to the conclusion that the only thing we could do was to try and find our own way out. It didn't sound easy. Then one day at the end of March, when mushy snow and clammy fog made Stockholm seem extra grey and wretched, we were told that we were all to be sent away to cut timber.

That evening the five of us sat in a room in the Norwegian hostel poring over an old atlas and conceiving vague plans. To begin with there was only the one thing on which we were all agreed: that we had not gone to Sweden just to chop wood. As the evening progressed, however, our ideas began to fall into line, and by the time we crept into bed we had all but achieved unanimity and there was a thick pencil line drawn across the old atlas. It ran right across European and Asiatic Russia and into China, from where there was a choice of two lines: one across China to Hongkong, and another over the Karakorum and Himalayas to the coast of India. In the ports and harbours of India and at Hongkong there are always Norwegian boats to be found. Both China and India look a reasonable size in an old atlas, and the names Karakorum and Himalaya do not sound so very intimidating when you read them on a map.

We felt that we were getting somewhere, and that the Swedes would have to get someone else to chop their wood.

The time that followed was a busy one. Chinese and Russian visas had to be obtained, and there were a thousand things about which we required information and enlightenment. Then, of course, there was the question of cash. We reckoned that we should need £150 apiece, and you don't find that lying about in the street, not even in Stockholm in wartime. That I was lucky enough to be able to go with the others was due entirely to the financial abilities of Andrew.

By some means or other, we tracked down a missionary who had been in China. He was a kindly man and gave us much good advice and a lot of information. Among many other things he told us that there was a caravan road from Alma-Ata in Russian Kazakstan, across the Tien Shan mountains to Kashgar in Sinkiang, and from there across the Karakorum and Himalayas into India.

To us Sinkiang sounded as good a place as any other, and we decided to have a closer look at that caravan road. It was that road we had in mind when we rigged ourselves out in riding breeches and high boots. Some difficulties over language we expected, but the others could speak a little German and English, so we hoped they would not be too great. It was only I who had stuck at the stage of being able to ask, 'Fred, where are you?' but not understand the reply.

I suppose there have been a few expeditions which set about their preparations with more foresight and knowledge, but I don't believe there can have been many which started out with greater expectations. Looking back on it now, it rather appears as though the whole idea was crazy, but is it laid down anywhere that the goddess of adventure lavishes her favours only on the sensible?

One day early in April we met at the aerodrome to go aboard the 'plane for Åbo in Finland. Soon we were soaring in the air above the Gulf of Bothnia. Below us lay mist, grey and woolly like an endless blanket, but above us the sky was clear and blue, and we accepted that as a good omen.

The train took us easily and painlessly from Åbo to Viborg; there we had our first skirmish with the Russian Passport Control—but everything passed off all right. Then, early one morning, we found ourselves on the platform in Leningrad, and there lay nearly five thousand miles of Soviet Russia ahead of us.

When you are young and green and stand on the threshold of a remote and foreign land, it is inevitable that half-forgotten things from the schoolroom crop up in your mind, things from books and newspapers, from the radio, and that these join together to form a picture. I must admit that my little bits of mosaic only produced a rather bewildering picture of Russia. It was like a double exposure, or as if two artists had each painted a picture on the same canvas, the one taking heaven for his subject, the other hell.

Imagine me, some days later, standing in the Red Square in Moscow trying to get some of it all to agree; and I was young and sufficiently unspoilt to feel my whole body tingling with the excitement of it.

There lay the Kremlin—okay. And Lenin's mausoleum. And the cathedral of St Basil. On that April afternoon the horizon was, in actual fact, almost cinnabar-red and the heavens heavily grey and Russian. But I saw neither troikas nor machine-guns. I just saw shabby taxis and lorries bowl-

ing across the Red Square, and very ordinary-looking
people bustling about. The noises were the ordinary ones of
motorcars and trams and the distant drone of factories
which was Moscow's melody.

I am always meeting people who want to talk about this
journey of ours, and few of them fail to ask what were our
impressions of Russia. That shows that there are many who
have a picture they would like tidied up a bit. But after
only a couple of days stay in Leningrad and Moscow and
then a railway trip straight across that large and remarkable country, one is naturally no cleverer than they. So,
as this story is supposed to be about things, people and
events that happened under more distant skies, I hope the
reader will excuse me if I cover the entire Soviet Union in
a couple of strides.

Let me just say that as we stood there on the platform in
Leningrad staring stupidly at a gang of women in thick
quilted but ragged clothes busy with picks and spades and
crow-bars digging a trench in the station precincts, and
thinking to ourselves: 'Aha! so that's how things are here,
is it!' suddenly up popped a representative of the Intourist
organization. He looked as though he for his part was
thinking: 'I'll give these sulky, piddling little capitalistic
chits something else to look at.' And so he drove us to a
fantastically elegant hotel—which was also called Intourist
—and showed us into an out-and-out princely suite: three
rooms and two baths and fine trappings.

We had a short nap and after that we made our first
acquaintance with Russian cooking—and enjoyed it. Then
a female of sorts who spoke Swedish came and took us for
a drive of several hours all round the lovely city on the
Neva. She must have thought that we were incorrigibly
capitalist, for while we drove along between statues,

churches, old palaces and new factories, we heard not a blessed word about Communism, but the girl never stopped jabbering about Peter the Great and Catherine the Second. Later, perhaps, she took fright and thought there had been a bit too much about czars and empresses, for we ended on the street corner at which the revolution started with a bang in 1917.

On the train to Moscow we were pretty crowded in our 'hard class' compartment, and when it is called 'hard' class in Russia, then hard indeed it is. Those wooden seats certainly were. As the train was more than overcrowded and the air 'on board' rather bad (to put it mildly) we had no great joy of that journey.

In Moscow, however, there was Intourist again, only this time the hotel was called Metropol. It wasn't quite so princely as Intourist in Leningrad, but nonetheless good and the food excellent. The crockery bore the czar's monogram.

Intourist offered to take us sightseeing, but we said 'no thank you,' and went for a stroll on our own in the centre where there wasn't a sign that the Bolsheviks have ever done anything since they came to power. We also saw a bit of the new factory and dormitory districts in the outer parts of the city, where there is no getting away from the fact that grey is Moscow's colour despite all its red flags. Then we went down into a couple of the underground stations and got a shock. To be honest, those huge light vaults with fresco paintings on the roofs and walls, and statues and carvings in niches along the platforms, and everything in lovely pure colours, were simply overwhelming. New York's subway and the London underground are poor and pokey in comparison.

All the Russians with whom we came in contact, whether

they were officials or private persons, always treated us with the utmost correctitude, were friendly and obliging. Further on in my travels I met Russians whom I have every cause to remember with gratitude for their goodness and helpfulness. Apart from that it is not easy to find anything to say about Russia, except what most people already know: that the Russians have a more difficult time of it than we do, and must work hard for comforts which we take almost for granted.

The Intourist man who accompanied us to the station when we went to get the train for Alma-Ata, asked us how we liked Russia. He was a decent chap, and we told him the truth: that it was a bit like the curate's egg, that the underground was mighty fine, but that we found no difficulty in restraining our enthusiasm at the sight of, for example, all the women engaged in hard physical labour which haunts you everywhere. He smiled and said that he could well understand that we saw it that way. 'But', he added, 'first we must become strong, then the luxuries will come. In time all Moscow will become like the underground.'

Not a bad programme. But what about people's time off?

Moscow's east station is like most east railway stations: old and grey, shabby and dismal. The seething crowd in the station hall was an immediate reminder that we were on our way out of Europe. Consonants swirled round our ears and the people sat in clusters with their bundles, parcels and belongings. Many of them had a number of round loaves with holes in the middle threaded on a string: their provisions for the journey.

Our tickets were for the hard class. To say that the train was crowded, is far too mild a description of the crush.

We had a journey of seven days ahead of us, and after counting and recounting our resources we had our tickets changed to 'soft class'. Of course, we could not really afford such luxury, but we gave way to the temptation and so we had a beautiful compartment to ourselves.

Away we chugged eastwards across the endless plains. The only break in the monotony was when the train occasionally stopped at a station. Every station in Russia had gigantic pictures of Lenin and Stalin, and a loudspeaker which emitted the most hellish row. Otherwise we had to make the time pass with a pack of cards and a set of chessmen. In the restaurant car none of the languages Andrew and Kai spoke were of any use, and all we could do was to find somewhere to sit, point to our mouths and say 'yum-yum'.

To begin with the fields were all covered with snow, but gradually it became warmer, the snow disappeared and soon the work of spring was in full swing wherever the ground was tilled, and the land there was arable for as far as you could see on either side of the railway line. We saw the tractors like tiny specks dotted about the plain, but here and there they were ploughing with horses too. Oxen were also being used, and soon we had our first sight of a long string of brown hump-backed camels swaggering across the steppe.

We passed Orenburg and knew that now we were out of Europe. By the following day, when we got a few glimpses of the greyish-blue expanse of Lake Aral, the heat had become ghastly. It was springtime, and while we sat there sweating and dreaming of an Easter trip on skis across the clean snows of Norway, the train trundled on across the steppe and into the capital of Kazakstan.

Alma-Ata, 'Father of Apples', is a large, strange and

lovely city lying in a fine fertile countryside to the north of
the Tien Shan. From having been the commercial centre
of an agricultural and fruit-growing district, Alma-Ata has
developed within a few years into an important link in the
chain of Soviet industrial expansion. Gigantic blocks of
dwellings made of glass, steel and concrete stand there
side by side with low mud huts and great smelting furnaces
and factories.

According to our friend the Swedish missionary, it was
here that we were to find our caravan road. We were
heartily sick of trains and looked forward to getting astride
some old nag and cantering away. Andrew, Sverre and Kai
took it in turns to reconnoitre, but none of them managed
to get even a sniff of that caravan road. There was a lot of
talk of an air route, and after a great deal of discussion and
weighing of pros and cons, the end of it all was that we
decided to go back to our railway.

This time it was hard class again. We got out at a station
between Alma-Ata and Novo Sibirsk, it was called Sarusck
if I remember rightly, and from here we went on by
lorry across a plateau to a fine little town called Tsjarkent.

Here Kai began to feel queer and his temperature shot
up. However, we carried on across the plain—which now
was no longer luxuriant and fertile but the next best thing
to desert. Then, when we reached Xiptoc, we realized to
our horror that Kai was seriously ill. We managed to get
hold of a doctor and he immediately pronounced it pneu-
monia and sent for an ambulance from Tsjarkent where
there was an hospital. I have not seen Kai since, but in
Bombay I learned that he had been there before me and
had gone to England. Thus he must have gone west again
and made his way through Iran.

Well then, that has brought us to Xiptoc, and it only remains to explain the musical instruments and the champagne.

In Leningrad we had exchanged a good many dollars into roubles, and then in Xiptoc we suddenly discovered that we were left with a whole heap of roubles which some one or other persuaded us we should be unable to use outside of Russia. The Russians had no objection to acquiring dollars, not in the least. But roubles into dollars? No thank you, can't be done! So we racked our brains and came to the conclusion that we must just comb Xiptoc for anything worth buying to take with us. This resulted in the litter of curious objects that lay strewn about the earthen floor.

We had a fine time of it in Xiptoc, and it was a likeable lot of people the Russians had sent there to look after that eastern frontier post. There was some fuss with our passports and they had to send a telegram to Moscow. As a result of that we had to wait there three or four days.

We still found language a bother when we wanted to eat, but when we ordered our farewell meal in Xiptoc we were served by a chap who knew a little more than just his northern tongue. Andrew told him that we were as hungry as wolves and wanted lots of food—'plenty food'. Obviously the Russian had made up his mind that no one was going to go about saying that you starved in Russia—not if he could help it. First he brought us a good thick soup, and bread to go with it, then roast chicken and potatoes and piles of vegetables, then eight—no exaggeration—actually eight eggs apiece. After that we had fruit salad and ended up with a stout glass of vodka.

When we finally did get away from Xiptoc, it was on a post lorry sitting on its load of sacks. Two Red Army men saluted stiffly at the frontier boom as we drove past on to the sacred soil of China.

2. Comrade Shun's Republic

AFTER DRIVING for an hour or more along the bad road which led from the Russian frontier, we reached the small village of Shimpanse where there was a customs house and a small garrison.

We jolted on down the one and only street, lined on either side with low mud houses. Horses and cows walked about with an air of venerability, and the men sat in clusters squatting in the street, chatting and enjoying themselves. They took life with crushing calm. Our lorry stopped outside the post office and the postmaster greeted us—our first official contact with Mother China. That old man in wide trousers and low-hanging jacket of some black cotton material with red butterflies on it, wearing a flat cap with a long silk ribbon on his head and embroidered slippers on his feet, was courteous and gracious as was to have been expected of a son of the Celestial Kingdom. His yellow old face was almost in the sand when he bowed in greeting and he produced a long rigmarole which we took to mean that he was pleased to see us.

'*Ka-ku-kao, la-li-lao—pa-pi-pao,*' said he, or what sounded like that; and we replied:

"Morning, old boy, nice to meet you.'

At that he realized we were foreigners and started the ceremony all over again, only this time he had a try with a long stream of Russian-sounding consonants. Even so that left us none the wiser, but a Chinese postmaster's sense of hospitality is as tough and indestructible as a dog's skin, and there was nothing for it but to follow him into his office. The old man clapped his hands and, hey presto! there was the slight figure of the postmistress standing in front of us with tea.

She, too, said '*ka-ku-kao*' and '*li-la-lao*', and the only difference between her dress and her husband's was that her jacket was shorter and she did not have a cap on her pyramid of lacquer-black hair.

The postmaster produced cigarettes and it was all very cosy. If the conversation had a tendency to come to a stop, that was not unnatural, for we were rather impatient to have the business with customs and passport control over and done with and be on our way again. After a deal of talking at cross-purposes we realized that here in China it was not possible to get everything done in one day, and with the kindly help of the postmaster we found ourselves somewhere to stay.

Before we got so far, however, an officer had come and had a look at our passports, the mere sight of which showed him that we were suspicious characters requiring two of his men to keep an eye on us. These two soldiers, who had black uniforms, a broad leather belt round their waists and high boots, were armed with blunderbusses with long terrifying bayonets of Russian design, and they were installed in a room next to ours in our Russian host's little mud house.

It was quite cosy in our room: the floor was of trodden earth, the walls whitewashed clay and the roof thin wood laths woven together rather like a flag-basket. There were two tiny windows set low in the walls which were decorated with pictures of Lenin and Stalin, and one of a slant-eyed, fierce-looking creature in uniform who, at that time, meant nothing to us, but with whose illustrious name and title we very soon became familiar.

Our host was obviously determined not to be behind the postmaster in hospitality, with the result that there too we received an incredible number of poached eggs apiece. After the meal he fetched a gramophone and played Russian songs for us. We were shamed into producing a bottle of champagne, and that put the Russian in an even better mood. As no Russian can be in a good mood without singing, the gramophone was soon shoved aside and one of our mandolines picked up and tuned. So we spent yet another evening nodding to the nostalgic melodies of the steppes.

The Chinese Customs and Passport Control are perhaps not as thorough and exact as to bother you, but they take a long time. It took us two days to get clear of Shimpanse, and when at last we were ready to leave and had clambered up on to the top of the cases and odds and ends that constituted our lorry's load, we discovered that we were to have a military escort. There was one soldier and one officer, the latter wearing a bandolier with a huge pistol stuck in it, a five-pointed red star on his shiny peaked cap, and a lot of dangling things which presumably were decorations. Apart from ourselves there was a poor shabby wretch with a great iron chain and a heavy ball fettered to his leg —most obviously a prisoner.

The well-decorated officer was one of the blandest peo-

ple I have ever seen. At all times he had a captivating
happy smile nailed to his face. He introduced himself with
a patter of queer sounds which none of us could interpret,
and so we just called him Chimpanzee.

We waved farewell to the village and away we went out
over the plain again. After we had been jolting along for a
bit we could see the snow mountains of the distant Tien
Shan away in the south. There were some queer formations
among them making it look like a wall with round and
square towers, and the lovely colours of it made us think
of home—and so we began singing a Norwegian song.

I will not pretend that we had made much progress
with our singing since our début in Xiptoc, but Chimpanzee thought it very nice, and no sooner had we stopped
than he leaped to his feet and began to 'render' a Chinese
ditty. To my mind a quartet of tom cats in the month of
March make divine music by comparison with that appalling row.

Our immediate goal was the town of Kuldsha some
seventy or eighty miles from Shimpanse. Here and there
we saw a few bushes and occasional trees out on the
steppe; now and again we rattled past herds of cows and
horses, flocks of sheep and goats, and in between we saw
people ploughing with seven or eight oxen harnessed to
the plough.

Just before we got to Kuldsha we drove past an aerodrome and noticed a few light-blue two-engined fighters.
The road was excellent in the vicinity of the town. We
drove along past low mud houses, some of them lying three
or four or more in a cluster with a three-foot wall round
the lot. Then we drove down an avenue of poplars, found a
hole in a wall and crept through it. With that we were
inside the town proper.

Outside the police-station we were surrounded by a bevy of soldiers whose eyes almost popped out of their heads when they caught sight of us. It looked as though it were our boots which caused the greatest sensation of all. The smiling Chimpanzee evidently considered that the time had come for him to show how dignified he could be, for he was as stiff and upright as a fighting cock when he signed to us to come down and follow him inside.

So far we had only seen mud houses of one storey, and compared with these the police-station was truly impressive: two whole storeys, mouldings painted red, whitewashed walls, and the whole graced with a huge red flag and a star of the same colour.

Inside, we were received by an officer who, judging by his badges, was undoubtedly of very high rank. He shook hands with us individually, saying: 'How do you do?' Then, after polishing his spectacles, inspecting our passports and considering at some length what he was going to say, he ordered the Chimpanzee in English that even I realized was pretty peculiar, to take us to the best hotel in the town. He saw us to the door and shook us by the hand all over again, and no doubt it was that mark of respect which caused all the loose soldiery to stand to attention and salute as we marched out of the police-station yard at the heels of the Chimpanzee.

There was an appalling commotion at the hotel on our account. Obviously we were to have the very best room in the place, and three or four members of the staff set about getting it ready with a great deal of shouting and bawling. To our intense delight Andrew had to start immediate inquiries as to the whereabouts of the w.c. To begin with the Chinamen had no idea what he was driving at. But it was becoming important for Andrew to get the information fairly soon, and so he squatted down and began grunting and groaning desperately. At that the penny dropped with the quickest witted of the little yellow men and he conducted Andrew into the hotel yard.

The hotel was one of the few houses in Kuldsha, other than the police-station, to have two storeys. It was built on a corner so that its two wings formed two sides of a rectangular courtyard. In both wings each storey had a veranda opening on to this courtyard, and these verandas were also used as sleeping places. In the centre of the courtyard was the enclosure to which Andrew was conducted shortly after our arrival. It was a sanitary installation deserving of more detailed description.

Some planks had been used to form the three sides of a small quadrilateral. The boarding was neither so high nor so close as to act as a screen. Inside this was the installation: a hole in the ground, and over this two planks on which you were supposed to stand. Later I was to learn that in certain villages deeper in Sinkiang the system had been considerably simplified. In some places it was the boarding which had been found superfluous, elsewhere they had even dispensed with the two planks as well.

Did I mention the flies?

Ugh!—with a suitable weapon you could easily have killed two thousand of the delightful creatures at one blow.

But our room was okay. Corner room on the ground floor. The corner in the direction of Kuldsha market-place had been sliced off and there was a door leading on to an open balcony. Orchestra stalls, neither more nor less. The room was furnished with four beds, four stools and a table. In the ceiling was a naked electric light bulb and electricity came from a coal-burning power station in the town which functioned for a couple of hours every evening. It did not matter that the low windows had no curtains—the layer of dust on them most effectively prevented the inquisitive from looking in.

The time came when we felt we wanted to eat. We discussed the possible menu and agreed that we would ask for milk and eggs and whatever else the house could provide. Then we got hold of a man we thought most resembled a head waiter and started negotiations.

Atle and I got the milk fixed. Down I went on all fours: Moo! Moo! while Atle squatted beside me and gave a talented imitation of a dairy-maid. Sverre and Andrew were to see to the eggs, so they hopped about now on one, now on two, legs and crowed and cackled: Chuck, chuck! Chook, chook!

The head waiter was not fool enough to talk Chinese when foreigners came to his establishment.

'*Charasho!*' said he and spat a great gobbet on the floor.

We got our milk all right, but instead of eggs we had roast chicken.

Anyway, the food was both good and plentiful but we were rather taken aback when we discovered that our cutlery consisted of two chopsticks each. But in Rome you must do as the Romans do, we are told; it was an art that had to be learned and our spirits at the table were not depressed because of it.

Well, such was our first evening in Kuldsha. We were, of course, rather inclined to wonder why we had been honoured with military attendants—they were in the adjoining room—yet we went to bed fully convinced that the next morning would see us off again heading for Canada.

How little we knew the tempo of Sinkiang! And who

could have dreamed that most of the summer would have passed before I should be able to shake the dust of Kuldsha off my feet?

The expression 'time is money' has no currency east of Shimpanse. In Sinkiang the very idea of time did not seem to exist. There people just sit placidly on their backsides and let things happen. Whether they happen today, tomorrow or in a hundred years, seems a matter of no concern whatever to these eastern gentry, at any rate to such as have wangled themselves jobs in the so-called administration or in the police.

You often hear it said that, compared with the European, the Chinaman's great virtue is his patience. And no thanks to him for it. In Sinkiang you are forced to learn patience if you want to keep going.

Our first lesson in this noble art took the form of having to wait eight days before we were told why we were not allowed to proceed.

Sverre was the first to blow up. Fuming, he announced that the swine were damn well going to out with it. He was going to the police-station and he was not coming out again alive until he had found out what those squint-eyed devils were up to.

He came back all right, and by no means as cocky as when he set out. He had the following pleasant little tale to tell us:

The Chinese Legation in Stockholm which had given us our visas, represented Chiang Kai Shek's government. In Sinkiang, however, where we happened to be, that Generalissimo had no authority whatever. Here it was General Shun do Bahn who had all the say in things. (Maybe the man was called Bahn do Shun, or perhaps it was Shan do Buhn or

Buhn do Shan—perhaps none of my versions are correct
but at least they include all the really important letters, I
feel sure of that.)

Sinkiang had become an independent republic for which
—and this much was quite clear—our visas were not valid.
Also it depended entirely on this same famous General Shun
whether we might have fresh ones and be allowed to
continue on our way.

This eminent personage apparently had his residence in
Tihua, also called Urumchi, the legendary capital of the
province, and this lay the best part of seven hundred miles
deeper into Asia. To Urumchi our passports had been sent
for inspection and possibly gracious renewal of the visas.
The perspicacious reader will realize that this inevitably
took time.

So there we sat! With something to chew on indeed! Of
course, Chiang Kai Shek's legation in Stockholm had known
full well that it was Sinkiang we had to go through, but
presumably they had not known about Comrade Shun and
the new state of affairs. Perhaps one had no right to expect
them to concern themselves with such a purely local event
in their own country. After all, China is pretty large, and
Sinkiang merely covers one million five hundred thousand
square kilometres and so is not much more than four times
the size of Norway.

We recovered again, or at least felt considerably better,
when we heard that we were to consider ourselves as the
general's personal guests and that in the fullness of time
his car would be sent to fetch us.

It was obvious that we had made a good impression on
the local authorities and were considered respectable. Our
guard was soon dispensed with, and we were able to roam
about Kuldsha free and unhindered.

3. Kuldsha

SINKIANG, or Chinese Turkestan, is surely the most sequestered of all the provinces of China. It is, perhaps, the least accessible and the least known of any territory in Asia with the one exception of Tibet.

The greater part of the province lies within the clasp of the mightiest mountain chains of Central Asia: in the south, towards Tibet and India, lie the Kwen-lun, Himalayas and Karakorum; to the west and north lies the thousand-mile range of the Tien Shan screening it from Soviet Russian territory. Nor are communications eastwards with its mother country, China, such that control commissions can be very frequent, for there lies the Gobi Desert.

Only a small part of Sinkiang, that in the north-west, lies outside this ring of mountains and desert. This is the Dzungaria plateau lying north of the Tien Shan, the westerly part of which is called the Ili plain or Ili valley, and that was as far as we had got.

The greater part of the population of Sinkiang lives in oasis towns and villages along the rivers, and a smaller

part as nomads up in the mountains where they roam about
with their flocks. Most of the towns lie to the south of the
Tien Shan and to the north of the Kwen-lun round the huge
desert called Takla Makan, the Wilderness of Death. Later
we shall make acquaintance with several of the towns and
take a sniff or two at Takla Makan itself.

Sinkiang's history is one of much blood and vicissitude.
Tibetans and Mongols, Huns, Tungus and Chinese have
taken one another's place as its lords. Each time the country
has changed hands, heads have rolled, for one and all seem
to have had the same motto: *Kalti bajskal* (Off with his
head!) For the last few centuries it has been predominantly
the Chinese who have had control of the province. After a
revolution in 1934-35 it became a sort of Communistic
republic, and when I was there, which was in 1941, I had
the very definite impression that Soviet influence was
strongly in the ascendant.

For the time being, however, let us have a look at
Kuldsha.

The rivers Tekes, Kunges and Kasj, which all come down
the northern slopes of the Tien Shan, unite to form the river
Ili which, sluggish and burly, flows westwards across the
uplands, trickles on across the steppes of Kazakstan and
ends its days in Lake Baikal. Some distance west of where
Kasj finds her two sisters, the town of Kuldsha has grown
up.

Canals for collecting water have been dug in a wide circle
round the town. From these canals others run radially in
towards the centre, and from these runs a confusion of lesser
ditches criss-crossing the rice-fields. On the outer fringes of
the circles you will see sheep, cows and horses grazing.
Beyond that again lies the plain, naked and greyish-white
from its clay and sand.

The banks of the canals are sparsely grown with tamarisk bushes, and here and there a willow or a slender poplar reaches up towards the sky. Nearer in towards the town there are fine orchards, and some of the poplars in the avenues can be quite tall and convey an impression of grandeur and dignity. That, though, is an impression of which you are soon disabused when once you are inside the giant ant-heap that is Kuldsha itself. For the most part the town consists of an interminable confusion of small rickety and wretched mud houses.

Apart from the police-station and the hotel there are not many houses in Kuldsha of more than one storey. And those there are more or less all bear the hallmark of the public building: red mouldings, red stars, red flags. As for the hotel, it is best we stop using the term at all, now that we have got to Sinkiang. There it is called 'serai' or 'karavan-serai'; and there are not many of the Sinkiang serais, I am sure, that can offer the same conveniences as those we enjoyed in Kuldsha. As a rule a serai is a long, low house with sheds outside for camels, horses and donkeys, and bedrooms which are little more than small hutches with mud bunks to lie on.

The usual, in fact almost the only, building material is mud, which may be mixed with straw, rushes and cow-dung. Here and there a bit of poplar stick protrudes out of a wall indicating that the mud has been laid over a sort of framework. In the business quarter in the centre, or the bazaar streets as we ought to say now, most of the houses had no wall at all on the pavement side; instead they had a wooden shutter to put up, or a tattered curtain to pull across. The word pavement, too, is a misnomer, for no such thing existed. However the best drinking dens and shops had a wooden affair put down outside their premises over the muddy street which was always liberally strewn with the dung of cow, horse, donkey, camel, hen and various other animals. The flat roofs of the houses were often prolonged over the street in a sort of awning.

The population of Kuldsha must lie somewhere between one hundred and one hundred and fifty thousand—perhaps nearer the latter. As befitted a town of that size the bazaars could satisfy needs of all kinds: fruits, vegetables, rice and maize; dangling copper goods and tinsmiths' wares; sugar, tea and salt; capes, shawls and motley cloths and rugs. Then there were the animal bazaars where donkeys, horses and other beasts changed hands. And the bakeries, whose numbers were legion, and whose owners always seemed to be squatting by the little charcoal stoves on which they baked their round stodgy-looking loaves.

Of course there were other things which were bought and sold. Including women. But that was not a traffic for the bazaars.

Horses, cows and hens wandered freely about the streets, taking sudden fright when a solitary lorry came chugging along. So too did the flock of Moslems always to be found sitting on their behinds in the mud swapping tall stories; reluctantly they would get to their feet and move aside a bit, and the mudguards on the prehistoric Ford would flap like the wings of a wounded crow as it went spluttering past.

The bearded stalwarts who came riding along on shaggy ponies were presumably Kalmuks or Tadshiks from the Tien Shan mountains. You could see an old crone come bumping along astride a great ox, followed by a man, presumably her husband, riding a saddle-backed cow. Away down the street you might see a Moslem gliding along with a long-eared ass between his legs.

Thin, slant-eyed, round-shouldered Chinamen and deep-chested Russians in long blouses and felt boots, together comprised perhaps ten per cent of the weird swarm of humanity in the streets of Kuldsha. The rest I must lump under the word: Moslem. For those Turkis, Turguts, Tan-yans, Tadshiks, Kalmuks, Khirgiz and whatever it is they are called, are one and all Moslems, faithful adherents of the Prophet, Allah's devoted sons.

The correct dress of the Moslem, even when it is ninety degrees in the shade, is a roomy, thick, lined cloak and high boots. Round his waist he winds a long broad piece of cloth, the *belbar*, and into that he sticks purse, pouch, knife and all the other things which he cannot do without. On his head he has a small cap of velvet or silk embroidered in all the colours of the rainbow, and this clings as tightly to his close-shaven skull as would a sliced rubber ball.

Such a Turkoman, when he is well dressed, can look rather splendid, especially when sitting astride a glossy chestnut stallion; but the poor Turkoman will often lack the elegant *belbar* and have a bit of rope round his waist instead. And the horses are often pretty mediocre too. The mass of the people, however, consists of those who have no horses. They potter about, slouching along in cotton breeches which are luxuriantly roomy at the back and skin-tight at the knee and round the legs; and you cannot say that they are well dressed.

Otherwise clothing is so varied that it is difficult to imagine a material which is not used. There is no end to the people's inventiveness which is especially impressive in the matter of headgear. Some wear claret-coloured objects like a small bucket with long feathers attached, others have huge skin caps like towers which must have needed a medium-sized bearskin apiece to make, and there are black turbans, white turbans, red turbans and parti-coloured turbans, and many other queer things.

But it is in more than just his clothes that the Moslem proclaims his individuality. If there is one thing about which the Turkoman is particular it is his moustache and beard. You can see well-groomed and well-waxed flowing moustaches as long and as thin as pack-thread; there are optimistically bristling baby ones of just three or four hairs on either side, or elegantly arching swallow's wings sprouting from beneath a hawk-like nose; there are symmetrical chin-tufts and an endless variety of combined beard and moustache by means of which the Turkoman emphasizes the fact that he is an individualist. Those you see going about with what looks like a badly worn broom on their faces will undoubtedly be Kalmuks or Khirgiz from the mountains, and they are not people of refinement.

The Turkoman shopkeeper has a decided business talent. His watchful eye sifts the passers-by in search of a possible customer, but he is not, like his counterpart south of the Himalayas, so avid as to demean himself by waving his arms or shouting or making a fuss. Like everybody else in Sinkiang he has mastered the art of being patient.

We stopped to watch one of these merchants discussing the price of a *belbar* with a customer, but as there seemed little chance of their reaching agreement, we strolled on.

An hour later we again walked past that same spot and the discussion was still going on. I imagined that later still there might be a pause in the proceedings while the merchant invited the other for a cup of tea behind the counter. Having taken their time over that, they would resume the discussion where they had left off. Finally, perhaps, the customer would renounce the idea; he didn't think he would have the *belbar* after all. Smiling his most ingratiating smile the shopkeeper would bow him out and look round for the next customer.

Much as I would like to be able to tell of how the Moslems live behind the curtains of their mud houses, or what it is like under the green trees in the gardens of the elegant houses of the well-to-do, I can do neither for I never had the chance to get inside.

Comrade Shun and his stalwarts were Communists. Unfortunately I cannot answer even such obvious questions as how far the Communist system had developed in Sinkiang. Had the fortunes of the rich Moslems, for example, been confiscated? I do not know for certain, but I imagine that they had not. I don't believe that Shun and Co. had got much farther than the stage of feeling most important in their offices and loving being able to be cocky and to cover themselves with red stars. Perhaps they went as far as to collect a few taxes now and then, and as long as they were able to do that they probably didn't give a damn what the lousy Turkomans did.

And the Turkomans? Were they happy people who felt themselves oppressed by the uniformed Chinese and who longed to be free as a nation? I don't believe that either. Rather, I should say the truth is that the different groups had no feeling whatever of solidarity one with the other, whether as a people or a nation. And that it was a matter of utter indifference to them whether it was Shun do Bahn or a representative of Chiang Kai Shek who sat in Tihua brooding over the red seal of power—as long as they were allowed to live their Moslem lives in peace.

And that Moslem way of life is just to sit on your behind and watch your food growing in the ground and occasionally utter a squawk or two to Allah. To be happy the Moslem must occasionally be able to do a fellow over a horse deal, he must be able to go without washing—other than dipping the tips of his fingers into a little water when he is going to pray to Allah—and there must be no interference in his loving and beating of his women, and he must be able to buy them and sell them again or swap them for a couple of old donkeys or a riding-whip, if that's the way he feels.

But the Moslem has his own worries where women are concerned: in recent years the demand has been greater than the supply and prices are absolute black market ones.

Yet perhaps the most important point of any description of Kuldsha should be—the flies. I am inclined to believe that not more than one in a thousand of the world's flies lives outside Sinkiang. All the others buzz about in that province which has long since been abandoned by both gods and decent people.

When Kuldsha's best serai was built it was not in the expectation that it would ever have to harbour guests so unreasonable as to demand fresh air at night. The windows in our room were not to be opened, and they were also fairly stoutly framed by local standards. Sverre, however, took the matter in hand and, he not being one to give up lightly, the windows were opened.

When we awoke next morning, we realized that in Kuldsha there were other things we must think of than just our lungs' desire for fresh air. The whole room was covered with a thick layer of dust. It was almost an inch thick on the table by the window. Evidently the wind had got up during the night. After that we had to consider the meteorological outlook before we could allow ourselves the luxury of open windows.

In the old days the monetary system of Sinkiang had been a complex affair with *miska, tenga, pul* and other peculiar things. Now, however, it has been simplified to mere dollars and cents. Our funds were in dollars and cents too, but American, and we had to set about getting some exchanged into the local variety. Our hunt for a financial institution brought us to a kindly person who most unexpectedly spoke English.

'Indeed,' said he, 'you will understand that in Kuldsha the bank's okay, but the people in it are a set of corrupt swine who will undoubtedly seize the opportunity to take a fat commission for themselves. Now, as it happens, I have a bit of cash in hand and I'll gladly exchange you a few at the full rate: five Sinkiang dollars to one American. In the bank you won't get more than four.'

Naturally we were touched by such kindness and changed quite a number of dollars. We discovered the rate later to be eight to one.

Money was becoming a bit of a problem altogether, partly because we had on occasion gone a bust which we could not afford, and partly because we had experienced so many delays on which we had not reckoned. Our resources had dwindled alarmingly and we unanimously decided to adopt a simpler way of life. After that there were no more grand orders placed with the serai's head waiter, a fact which unfortunately did considerable damage to our reputation. We even became so spartan in our ways that for a time we ate only once a day, and then the menu comprised little but stodgy dumplings which were the cheapest thing we could find.

For some reason or other we all began to have trouble with our tummies, and our visits to the courtyard became alarmingly frequent. Andrew went into the town and found what looked like a chemist. The label on the bottle with which he returned was in Chinese, and we were not quite certain whether it was a specific for lice or stomach upset, so the trial period was quite exciting. Happily the drops had the right effect.

I think that it would be correct to say that we were a bit of a sensation in Kuldsha. It seemed to be our boots that people found particularly fascinating. In the end our popularity became so great that we had to give an interview to a reporter from one of the local Chinese newspapers. He was a bit of a linguist and very free with his '*Charasho, tovaritch!*' 'Okay, gentlemen!' and '*alte Kameraden.*' He too seemed to be bewitched by our boots and he hinted that if any of us would consider selling he could get a block of houses in Kuldsha for them. But there was nothing doing.

It was from him we learned that we were known all over the town as the 'Anglees with the shiny boots'. In that part of the world they only recognized two categories of foreigner: Russians and Anglees (or Englishmen). Any idiot could see that we were not Russian, and so we were English.

When our conversation had been in progress for some considerable time and we had been told that we were the first Anglees ever to have come to Kuldsha from the west, the reporter skilfully manoeuvred us on to another subject:

Didn't four fine fellows like us find it a bit boring being in Kuldsha so long without female company?

It was by no means easy to know whether that was a kindly offer to provide us with introductions to feminine society in Kuldsha, or just an opening gambit in an out-and-out business offer. Far be it from me to suggest that any of us were as stoutly virtuous as the famous Joseph, but we had seen something of the local beauties. And then the lice on all the Moslems' beards! There was a limit to everything!

I still regret not having got hold of a copy of the *Kuldsha Herald* or whatever the paper was called which carried our interview. He must have made a good thing out of the four long-distance tourists who were so filled with wonderment at the lovely and well-administered city on the Ili. And he no doubt made us say, as all tourists must, how we admired the wonderful social services the authorities had provided.

Should you have got the impression that we occupied ourselves largely with the study of sociological problems, I must disabuse you of it, for our thirst for knowledge was not as great as that. We spent a lot of our time on amusements. Among other things we went to the cinema.

Yes, there was a cinema in Kuldsha and, what is more, the largest I have ever seen. The performance took place in the open, the white screen being hung up on a wall. The management had saved itself the cost of benches or chairs and all unnecessary equipment like that, so you sat on the ground. The area was marked off by bushes and a ticket cost fifty cents. The films were Russian.

Despite all its sights we gradually found ourselves getting bored with the centre of the town, and so one day we went for a walk in its surroundings. Out near the aerodrome we discovered to our amazement a proper sports ground. The surface was earth, but there were tufts of grass here and there, and though the track might not have been up to much in wet weather it was then dry and okay. The ground was surrounded with elegant rows of poplars and the whole place looked most attractive.

What attracted us most, however, was the sight of a flock of airily dressed Amazons playing basket-ball. We realized that they must be Russians and obviously owed their presence there to the aerodrome, where no doubt they had something or other to do.

At first the sight of these frisky strapping girls quite took our breath away, and if they had been a bit easier to make contact with, one or other of us might well have abandoned the virtuous role of Joseph. From then on our motto was 'Out of the town!'

When it was suggested that we make a trip to the Ili, the idea was immediately adopted. But it was a mile or two to the river and the heat in Kuldsha makes you lethargic. None of us wanted to walk so far.

What does one do in such a situation in such a place?

Naturally you take a cab.

There were plenty of them on the ranks with every degree of luxury and comfort, and fares that varied accordingly. They ranged from those consisting of two wheels and an axle with a few bits of planking over it, to four-wheeled landaus with bright silk upholstery. The smartest of them had stools to sit on, great parasols and lots of silk cushions and frippery. As for the motive power, you could choose between pure Arab, worn-out shaggy Khirgiz pony, heavy melancholy oxen, and cows with horns as long as a bad year.

We decided on one of the cheaper vehicles, not only for reasons of economy, but also because we thought the wonderful rugs and upholstery of the more expensive might be the hiding place of certain little stowaways who would seize the opportunity to move over to us and so get a free trip to Canada.

Thus we drove out of the town behind a filthy little pony. Like his lord and master he had learned to take life with supercilious calm.

The Ili was a good couple of hundred yards wide where we reached it. However, there was a ferry with some Russians working on it, and that ferry was one of the smartest I have ever seen. They had stretched a thick wire across the river, and to this two big barges were attached with their bows pointing upstream. They were attached to the wire by a system of blocks and wires and had planks fixed across them to keep them wide apart. In the space between the two barges they had arranged what looked like a large rudder and when this was turned to one side or the other by means of tackle, the current took the barges across the river. It was slow, but sure, and above all called for no effort, and that was the main consideration.

Kuldsha was obviously a growing town, and we acquired a slight insight into the way dwelling-houses are constructed in that part of the world.

When a Moslem has got himself his plot of ground, the first thing he does is to make a largish hole. Next he digs a trench to the nearest water channel and leads the water to his little hole. Having got so far he can now, instead of drawing up plans for approval and filling in forms of application for this and that, set about obtaining his materials. He gets hold of some flat wooden boxes. These he fills with earth, pours a little water on it, gives it a pat or two, and after the benevolent sun of Sinkiang has shone on for a bit, there he has some bricks. Then he makes a paltry frame of poplar sticks, and builds up his house on that. Between each layer of brick he perhaps lays some straw and twigs and pours a little water on it, but otherwise he pays little attention to angle or level. When he reaches the roof, he first spans the gap with some poplar sticks and branches, and over them stretches a rush mat. On top of this he puts a layer of earth eight or twelve inches thick and damps it. When the sun has dried it a bit, there is his house finished.

Meanwhile we had got into May. We had waited in Kuldsha for nearly two weeks already, and it seemed two weeks too many. We grew more and more impatient to hear what Comrade Shun had decided.

Since the day when Sverre had gone and raised hell at the police-station and learned about our visas, one of us had called there every day for news. And what extraordinarily different news we received. One day we were told: yes, it was all arranged and we should be able to continue on our way the following morning. The very next day we were told that they expected things to take a month yet. Then we were told that they thought we were bound to be sent back to Russia.

We could not make head or tail of it. All we could do was to wait and see.

4. Young and Ling

/\

ONE EVENING when we were out watching the people in
the market-place, we noticed two men standing staring at
us, two slim figures in officer's uniform of a quite different
kind to the usual Sinkiang variety. They came up and spoke
to us:

'How do you do?' said one.

'Are you English?' asked the other.

'No, Norwegian.'

'Ah, from Norway!'

It was the first time we had met anyone in Sinkiang who
had any idea such a country as Norway existed, so naturally
we pricked up our ears. The two introduced themselves as
Young Ying Nan and Ling Xao Kong, officers in Chiang Kai
Shek's Air Force. Both spoke good English. For certain
reasons I was rather out of the conversation, but I gathered
that the others were amazed by the questions the two asked
about our trip and the knowledge they showed of Norway.

'But Quisling has taken over the government in Norway,

and so Norway is on the side of the Germans, so to speak, isn't she?' they asked.

When Andrew and Sverre explained that Quisling had only a tiny clique of supporters, and that we had left Norway in order to join the Norwegian forces outside, their enthusiasm knew no bounds. When they heard of our troubles with our visas and General Shun and of our difficulties in getting on, they at once said that they would help us. The evening ended with their inviting us to dinner at the Restaurant Asia the following day.

The Asia proved to be run by two bland and well-nourished Russian women. Their patrons were almost all officers, and the few civilians there were all well dressed Moslems. By Sinkiang standards it was not at all a bad restaurant, even though it harboured so many flies that any European head waiter would have committed suicide. We went there in our gala dress, after spending all morning brushing clothes and polishing boots. It would be difficult to imagine better hosts than Young and Ling, and it was a most successful meal. The wines and the dishes were exquisite and numerous.

Don't think that in previous chapters I have overdone my descriptions of conditions in Sinkiang and have been a bit patronizing, but as we sat in that restaurant with two of Chiang Kai Chek's Air Force officers it was our turn to feel small and slightly inferior. After what we had seen in Kuldsha it felt very strange indeed to be sitting opposite those two whose whole manner and appearance spoke of a high and ancient culture. Both had that self-evident, indefinable assurance which you encounter so seldom in our race even among educated people.

And after all Young and Ling were fellow countrymen of all those other queer beings. That, perhaps more than anything else, made us understand what a huge and wonderful land China is.

It certainly gave us something to think about when they informed us that they had been sent up there by Chiang Kai Shek to act as instructors at an aerodrome inside General Shun's republic, a republic which had torn itself away from the mother-country in a civil war and which, together with other Communist provinces, had taken part in fighting against the troops of the Central Government itself. Even while at war with Japan they could occasionally find the time for a skirmish or two, and now, of course, we know that the fighting with Japan was hardly at an end before the two sides were at each other's throats again in full civil war.

It may seem as though I have on purpose contrasted these two first rate fellows of Chiang Kai Shek's with the ridiculous creatures serving General Shun but that is not so. It is mere chance that Young and Ling happened to come into the picture. Since then I have talked with people who were in China all during the war and who maintain that most of Chiang's divisions consisted of bandits of incredibly low standing and that conditions in many provinces of Central China were considerably worse that those I describe in Sinkiang. On the other hand I have heard both British and American journalists assert that the Communists came to power in the northern provinces because of the organizing ability of their leaders, and that they have effectively got rid of all corruption in the administration. Don't ask me where the truth lies! All I know is that China is a darned awkward country to get wise to.

Nonetheless, I am going to be rash enough to mention one or two things which I noticed.

The wearing of uniform was confined to persons of one definite racial type out of all those in Sinkiang's very mixed population. That was easy to see. The members of the army and police all had the distinguishing marks of the Chinese. Thus, for all his Communism, Comrade Shun was practising a sort of racial policy. Moslems of all kinds were kept out of it.

Nor was it hard to discover that it was the Russians the authorities took as their model, and that the Russians had considerable influence.

During my tribulations in that godforsaken republic I learned a magic formula, which I shall now reveal:

Should you ever come to Sinkiang in similar circumstances to mine and find yourself having trouble with the police or soldiery, pretend to be furiously angry. Roll your eyes, grind your teeth and trot out all the oaths and swear words you know. It doesn't matter what language or languages they are in, provided at the end you mobilize all your strength and roar in their yellow mugs: '*Konsulstovo Rossiskai*! !' Then, I assure you, even the most quarrelsome soldier will become as meek and obliging as a lamb.

I have no idea what Young and Ling did to help us, but, whatever it was, things began to move. Chimpanzee came in person to visit us at the serai, and, beaming more brightly than ever, informed us that we were to start for Tihua the following day. Were we glad!

It was now May 8th, and strangely enough it turned out that Chimpanzee's information was correct. After spending most of the following day waiting at the police-station, we did get away in the end.

Lorry again. Sacks and odds and ends and petrol tins and cases on the flat, and we were on top of it all. Chimpanzee was again in charge, and he clambered up to join us together with one of his men. The others squeezed in beside the driver.

Our spirits were high as we rattled out of Kuldsha. Cows sprang for their lives to avoid collision, and hens sought refuge in squawks and flapping.

Either that driver was quite unlike all the rest of the population of Sinkiang or perhaps, as sometimes happens, those people lose all their sedateness and sense of moderation as soon as they get behind a steering-wheel. However, never have I experienced such appalling driving. When we were well outside the town ill luck would have it that there was another lorry on the road ahead of us. That was more than our driver could bear to see. He pressed the accelerator to the floor boards and kept it there. We tore past that other lorry at a disgraceful speed. As our driver tried to pull the vehicle back on to the road he hauled on the wheel and the whole thing went over.

'Jump!' shouted Andrew.

I made a wild effort to take off, but I was sitting all wrong among the sacks, and then over we went. Something went 'twang' in my back, thousands of stars exploded in front of my eyes, and then all was darkness.

A little later I had the sensation that something was squeezing my chest most horribly. I had to work furiously to get my breath, my heart was going in jerky furious rushes, and then I fainted away again.

When I recovered consciousness once more, I saw Sverre's face close to mine. He looked appalling, for one side of his head was all bloody. Beyond him was Atle limping about clasping his head and his hip. Andrew was running from one to the other with a wild look in his eye, while Chimpanzee lay motionless at the side of the road, and one of the soldiers sat with blood pouring down his face. The lorry lay off the road with its wheels in the air.

'Willie's alive, but Chimpanzee's had it,' I heard Andrew say.

Then I shivered with fear as I realized that I was incapable of moving.

People soon came running up, and Andrew raved and shouted:

'Hospital! Doctor! Car! Quick, damn you!'

The police came. The driver, who, curiously enough was unhurt, was arrested and fettered by the leg. Then an ordinary private car appeared from somewhere, and Andrew lifted me into the back seat. Sverre and Atle were able to crawl in by themselves, and very slowly we were driven back to Kuldsha.

The courtyard of the so-called hospital swarmed with girls, and they had a stretcher. Andrew got me out of the car and I was carried off to the 'bath'. Andrew went to the washroom to help Sverre, and meanwhile the swarm of 'nurses' descended upon me.

I was lying in the 'bathroom', doubled up with my head in my lap and unable to move. Nor was I so very conscious of my surroundings. Round me thronged at least ten of the dirty scruffy females all aged between sixteen and eighteen, and all cackling away at the same time. It was a commotion comparable only to panic in a hen-run.

It was only when the girls set about getting the clothes off me that I realized my inside had emptied itself after the crash on the road. What a business!

The girls pulled and tugged at me, and with much howling and screeching I was dumped into the bath. There they scrubbed me and sluiced me with great thoroughness, while I hoped for a merciful swoon to help me out of that ignominious situation. But no! I was heaved up and back on to the stretcher, and the girls set off with me to another part of the building. There a grave man in a white coat came and examined me and gave me an injection. Half-asleep I was carried into another room where there were a lot of beds.

The girls came hurrying up with a bed which was placed with one end on a bedside table; the mattress was removed and three planks put in its place, and on that I was laid with a sandbag under my back. The serious doctor, who had a bald head and a heavy face, rigged up strappings from my shoulders to the head of the bed, and his smile was good and kindly as he said: '*Es muss gehen. Es muss!*'

I am afraid that the others got little out of me during my first few days in hospital. Sverre lay in the bed next to mine with his head enveloped in bandages, and now and again Andrew and Atle came and sat and tried to chat with me. They told me that the Russian doctor had said that three of my vertebrae had been knocked out of alignment, and that I should have to lie clamped on the sandbag for two or three months in order to get them back into place, but that he hoped I would be quite all right in the end. Atle was okay again and Sverre had got off more lightly than had at first been thought. He would be fit to travel in a few days. The police now were insisting that all three of them should get away to Tihua. It was obvious that they could not wait for me.

It wasn't a very cheering prospect, but all three bravely did their best to assure me that things would not be so bad. They were going to send telegrams all over the place. As soon as they got in touch with the first British or Norwegian authorities, whether in China or India, they would move heaven and earth to get help sent to me. They might even be able to have an aeroplane sent to fetch me. After all there was an aerodrome there.

On May 14th, Andrew and Atle left Kuldsha and Sverre followed them two days later. That left me alone and with plenty of time to think.

5. The Medical Services
of Sinkiang

Extract from Diary   *Kuldsha, May 17th*

Sverre has just left, and I have been moved into another room some thirteen feet square with a bed stuck in each corner. On the wall facing me is a doorway with a curtain, and between me and the Moslem in the other corner there is a tiny window-aperture.

I am having fewer injections now my temperature is down, and, as I hang here in my straps, I am gradually beginning to take an interest in my surroundings.

I am streaming with sweat even though I am lying stark naked under the sheet, which is the same sheet I was given when I came in a week ago. It's been sopping with sweat the whole time, and now it is no longer pleasant to touch. I bet it's over a hundred degrees in here. My back hurts a lot, and my head too. And my shoulders. My tummy's in the throes of revolution and it feels as though anything may happen.

I am thirsty, but the filthy water puts me off. I'm hungry too, but every time one of those filthy girls comes with food, it makes me vomit. Once a day one of them comes with soup, chicken soup with vegetables. The soup itself may be all right, but the girl brings it in a shallow enamel bowl really intended for washing instruments in and her filthy thumb demonstrates that the soup is not the least bit too hot. There are no spoons. You must lap it down as best you can. When the girl is serving one of the Moslems, she stands patiently there picking her nose while he has his soup, and then she pours out a fresh helping for the next man. Wash up? What a ridiculous idea! We are in Kuldsha! Occasionally we get a bowl of tea and a piece of dry bread. There are no plates. The girl brings the bread in her paw.

The stench in the room here? God knows if I can find the words to describe it. Nor can I speak of the flies. Five thousand of them. More perhaps.

The only thing we do not lack is female attendants. So far we must have had at least twenty in this room. I have discovered that there are three categories: first 'trained nurses,' then those who are still being trained, and lastly some weird beings called *najas*. They are only allowed to do the simpler jobs like taking food round and a peculiar procedure with bucket and long-handled broom which is called floor-washing.

There isn't one of them I can talk with. You might just as well sit by a pond full of croaking frogs and try to interpret their conversation as try to get any sense out of the peculiar noises that buzz about your ears here. It's only when the Russian doctor comes to visit us that I can exchange a few words with someone. I rack my brains for German words but my vocabulary is horribly meagre and the doctor is a very busy man. He is the only qualified doctor in all northern Sinkiang. Yet, when he pays me a visit, he still has time to go and fetch a towel and soap if he notices that I am sore from the straps. He washes me himself and rubs me with spirit, arranges the sand-bags and everything else, while the nurses just stand and gape.

I am beginning to grow fond of this sweet-natured Russian, and always I am on tenterhooks to learn whether he will shake his bald pate and say '*Nicht gut*!' or whether there will be a smile and a '*Besser*'.

And once when, rather diffidently I drew his attention to the dirty sheet, he flung out his hands in a sorrowful gesture:

'*Ja, ja, ja . . . aber wir haben nichts.*'

The poor wretch to the right of the door is obviously in a bad way, for his hands are in constant motion clutching at various parts of his belly. Anyone can see that it's his guts. And from his lips comes a perpetual muttering: '*Bebblelubbelupp . . . Allah il Allah . . . bubbelupp!*'

The fellow-sufferer on his left is not one to disturb anybody with untimely exclamation, yet any idiot can diagnose his trouble too: stomach trouble. For even though this hard-tried disciple of Allah keeps his lips most firmly closed and lies as motionless as a dead fish staring at the ceiling, he has another opening which aro-matically and phonetically proclaims to the world at large that the functioning of his intestines has gone wrong. The trumpet blasts come at regular intervals.

On my side of the room lies a Moslem who has nothing

but supercilious disdain for the two stomach cases. He is an old fellow with a hooked nose, just skin and bones. He's one of the beard and moustache fanciers. His black waxed moustaches are so long that they look like two snakes which have lain down on his chest and stuck their heads into one each of his nostrils.

I can't for the life of me discover what's wrong with the old boy. It looks as though he were a devotee of the Orient's contemplative life and busy winding up some mysterious ritual. As he lies there gazing extra thoughtfully into space, I can see his adam's apple sink down and and down towards his chest, but it must be hung on a piece of elastic, for suddenly it jerks up into his neck again and while the snakes follow suit, seeming to rear up to strike, the man's head slowly rises from the pillow, turns through forty-five degrees, and a gobbet comes whizzing in my direction and drops to form a fresh oasis in the dust on the earthen floor. The process is then reversed and the head restored to the pillow, the snakes relapse comfortably into place again and he gazes once more thoughtfully into space.

I try in vain to discover whether there is any connection between the intervals of his spitting and the noises from the other two. In the end I decide that the old boy must have been in Finland and that he is now trying to make a map of that land of a thousand lakes from memory.

In my loneliness I have only 'Auntie' in whom I can confide. She has two hundred good sides to her pages and cost me three shillings in a stationer's in Stockholm.

When I opened my diary today, I discovered that it was May 17th, Norway's Freedom Day. Not much freedom, of course, for anyone, and for me there was also the mournful ceremony of renunciation, for I had to bury the dream of the boy who returned to his country with its freedom, speeding up Oslo Fjord in a silver-glittering aeroplane. I realized that it was little use hoping that my back would ever be serviceable enough for me to be of use in the air. Tears on pale cheeks, I'm afraid.

But it's a poor soul that can't find some little dream for solace. The war must come to an end some time, and the Norwegian Air Force will do its bit in achieving victory. All right. But if there is to be fighting in the air, there must be hangars and somebody to keep them swept and clean. That's a thing you can do with a hump on your back, do so well that people say: 'By Jove, that chap can sweep a floor!'

'*Bubbelubbelupp* . . . *Allah! Gruuunnt* . . . *Allah il Allah!*'

The map of Finland grows larger and larger.

Sometimes one is nearer the top of the world, sometimes down; that's the way it is with most people. But that May day in Kuldsha was the only time I have been so far down as to be on the verge of self-pity. Once you start that, then, as everyone knows, it's all up with you. I didn't know much about anatomy, and as I lay there I just took it for granted that I should be a cripple for life.

I hung there in my straps in the stifling heat of Kuldsha, wiping the sweat from my face and inhaling the smell of Moslem till my nose wanted to go on strike. I remembered the clear frosty January night when I stood on the platform and said goodbye to my parents. And I remembered too, a saying of Dad's that it's always fun being alive just to see how life goes.

There's nothing very unusual in breaking your back and getting well again, and, if everybody who spent some months in hospital took to writing about it, the rest of humanity would have to set about building paper mills. But in Kuldsha hospital I witnessed a number of things which were not what you usually see in a hospital, and I think that I might as well say something about them.

It was decidedly one of the better rooms in which I lay, and most of my room-mates were operation cases. As a rule they were not in long before they took a trip to the operating department and returned unconscious on a stretcher. They were obviously hard up for beds, and as soon as they had to some extent recovered, they had to make way for the next person. On occasion we were quite a little league of nations; one Chinaman, one Russian, a Moslem and a Norwegian. Each time a bed became vacant I breathed a silent prayer that the doctor might send a Russian or a Chinaman, for neither smelt half so revolting as did the Moslems.

Those who know will tell me that the people of Turkestan are relatively clean compared with Tibetans and individual Chinese. This is based on the fact that the Turkoman's religion enjoins him to wash before he prays or takes a meal —which he does. I have not been in Tibet and Sinkiang is all I have seen of China, so what I have to say does not refer to China as a whole. And, to be quite truthful, I must admit that some individual Moslems were not really so bad at all. There were some who dipped the tips of their fingers in water and splashed a little on their faces now and again, and there were long rigmaroles addressed to Allah and much stroking of beards both before and after meals and at certain hours of the morning and evening, but most of them were appalling pigs. I stick to that.

The fully trained 'nurses' got a wage of ten Sinkiang dollars a month. Those who were being trained got nothing, and what a *najas* was given I have no idea, but it could not have been much for the hospital was not expensive: thirty-three Sinkiang cents, roughly three-pence, a day.

Nor did the *najas* take their duties very seriously. One day they would bring the main meal at twelve noon, the next day perhaps at nine o'clock at night. And it was always with a pert expression they handed you the tin bowl and said: '*Baksla, Sahib, tjashfiva* (Please sir, food).' In time I too acquired manners and smiled nicely back and said: '*Banjama* (Thank you).'

Gradually I got hold of a few words, but it did not amount to much for some of the girls spoke Turki, others Mongolian, others chattered away in Chinese or Russian and heavens knows what else besides.

All the *najas*, however, were indescribably dirty and scruffy, and they smelt of death and corruption. The worst of all was one called Mirosa; when she appeared on the scene you smelled nothing else.

It was as good as a play to see them 'do' the room. They came with a long-handled broom, a bucket with a little water in it and a bit of old sacking. They spent most of the day using the sacking to shove the dirt into the corners or under the beds. In the pauses—which were frequent and of long duration—they kept themselves busy picking their noses, blowing them in their fingers and scratching their heads.

Despite the appalling shortage of equipment of every kind, there really was a chamber-pot to every bed, and believe it or not, those pots were emptied and cleaned every day. A *najas* would come with a bucket; first she emptied all the pots, then she took them solemnly by the handle one by one and swilled them out in the mixture and put them back in their places again. Don't ask me whether she could keep track of which belonged to whom.

Occasionally there would be a poor devil who was reduced to the urine-bottle and that made matters far more complicated. There was only one in the hospital, and when needed it had to be searched for in one or other of the big wards. When you happened to have heard that venereal diseases were rife and virulent in that part of the world, you were darned thankful to be able to use a pot.

The nurses were, perhaps, a shade better than the *najas*, though even they were far from clean. Most were eighteen years of age, and bedmaking did not seem to have been included in their training.

As well as the Russian doctor, there were two other practitioners, if you like to call them that, both of indeterminate mixed blood. One was a decent chap with drooping moustaches, the other a repulsive fish who always went about with a sarcastic sneer on his face. All three had names which were quite impossible and I prefer just to call the Russian 'the Doc', and the others respectively 'the Moustache' and 'the Sneer'.

Being there was not as bad as you might think. You found various little ways of making the time pass: for example, a *najas* came to wash the floor and you could amuse yourself guessing how old she might be: fourteen, perhaps fifteen? Then you saw her legs and you knew that she was older than that. She couldn't have become so filthy in just fifteen years.

In the end I even succeeded in getting a fresh sheet. I kept pestering one of the nurses till she brought me a clean one. It happened that there was a bed vacant just then, and the dirty sheet from my bed was placed straight on that empty bed, and with that it was ready to receive the next Moslem. So don't come and try to tell me they didn't favour the European!

One Moslem patient spent some days there screeching to Allah; he was borne out and came back with bandages round his stomach. The nurse laid a sandbag over his stomach to keep him from tearing the bandage off while he was still under the anaesthetic. The nurse then departed and the man, who lay there moaning, nevertheless somehow tumbled the sandbag on to the floor. I was incapable of helping, and the other patients were completely uninterested. I had to shout for all I was worth before a nurse came in and the bag was put back in place. This happened two or three times, then the nurse grew angry and flung the bag under the bed. After that it was no use my shouting for no nurse came—and an hour or so later the wretched Moslem was on his way to his dear Allah. The Doc was furious when he came, and I never saw that nurse again.

One day they brought in a Chinaman who, judging by his clothes, must have been well-to-do. He looked dreadful, the poor wretch, and in fact he did not last long. His family had been warned and they were all there beside the bed seeing the old chap start on his long journey. That was how I happened to see the right and proper way of burying a Chinaman. First he was washed and dolled up and his hair done, they dressed him in the whole rig-out from the skin outwards, and then topped it off with a splendid coat with embroidery and silken-tassels. Nor, of course, was the three-cornered hat forgotten. Next came the coffin, painted all over with roses and Chinese characters, and twice the size of ours.

When the man had been laid among the cushions and

brocades in the coffin, the procession moved off. By then I was a bit tired and rather enjoyed the thought of having a little peace and quiet so that I could have some sleep. But there I was mistaken. Once outside there started the most awful hullaballoo with women wailing, screeching and howling. It went on the whole blessed night. Evidently they always engage a wailing chorus to help out when a Chinaman of any position shuffles off this mortal coil, and the extent of the concert is a measure of the departed's economic position.

The Doc was a decent chap. He was always adjusting my straps and had obviously sworn to himself that those vertebrae were going back into place whether they wished to or not. Now and again he would stop for a chat and with admirable patience spoke to me in German slowly and distinctly, so that I was able to understand and talk a bit with him. One evening he asked what it was like in Norway, and I tried to tell him a little of the way things were. He said that he was amazed that we were so well off— but, he added, in Russia many things were pretty good. He hoped in time to get more equipment and help from Russia, and in due course he would get his hospital ship-shape all right. You can say what you like about the Russians, but they don't lack courage in tackling things.

When I once asked him how he ever managed to operate with such an appallingly incapable staff, he replied that he had a few first-class people in the operating theatre. Evidently he wanted to prove to me that that wasn't just bluff, for shortly afterwards I received the shock of my life when in walked a young girl in a dazzling white apron, who set her head on one side and said: *'Guten Tag!'*

Her name was Lulia; she was eighteen and worked in

the operating theatre. I could scarcely believe my eyes when I saw a girl who was washed and clean. After that she came in for a chat quite often and she told me, among many other things, that the Doc was almost killing himself with work. Often he had three or four difficult operations a day, plus all the other things he had to attend to. Lulia told me too that there was a lot of sickness among the Turkomans: goitre, tuberculosis and venereal diseases being the most prevalent.

Then one day another girl came in and looked at me and smiled and said:

'*Guten Tag! Na? Wie geht's?*'

She was called Elizabeth Tanzen and she was of German origin. I realized that the Doc had moved her from another department for my sake. By Norwegian, or English, standards Elizabeth wasn't perhaps anything much to write home about, either in appearance or in her qualifications as a nurse, but for Kuldsha she was nothing less than a miracle. Not just because I could talk a little with her, but also because she did get things moving a bit.

Elizabeth spoke Russian as well as German, and my bedside became a language school. I got a lot of help from a German New Testament she gave me. She told me that once there had been a Norwegian missionary in Kuldsha. Torvik, he was called, and he had kept a school as well as doing missionary work, but after the revolution in 1935 he had had to leave.

The rest of the girls were hardly such as to trouble the peace of one's heart. The Chinese were somehow too thin and bony, and as a rule the Moslems were inclined to be lumpy and a bit too broad in the undercarriage. Yet nature has her caprices, and never have I seen a more striking example of that than seventeen-year old Mira Samorska, a mixture of Russian, Chinese and every kind of Moslem. Without any doubt whatever she was the loveliest girl I have ever seen. Ye gods. What a film face! If Hollywood had discovered her, even Ingrid Bergman would have been reduced to the ranks. Her huge eyes were just slanting enough to notice, her hair was black and shiny like a new car, and on the left side of her head she always wore a fresh, deep red rose.

6. Tanya Fyodorova

/\\.\/\\.\/\\.\/\\.\/\\.\/\\.\/\\.\/\\.\/\\.\/\\.\/\\.\/\\.\/\\.\/\\.\/\\.\/\\/

ONE DAY Elizabeth came and told me that they had got a new Russian sister and that she was going to come and pay me a visit. Once she arrived life really did become considerably easier; not just because she was clean and game and pretty and sweet—for she was all that and more too—but never in my life have I met anyone who looked so good and gentle as that eighteen-year-old Russian girl. She introduced herself as Sister Tanya Fyodorova, smiled and at once set about making my straps and the sandbag comfortable.

Another little Russian had come with her. She was called Maginor, and those two began a new era in our hovel. Dust and flies had a bad time of it, and the Moslems were always in hot water for spitting.

Tanya also spoke German and good Turki too, so now I really got down to learning. She was wonderfully good at drawing and whenever there was something I didn't under-stand, she drew it like lightning with her pencil. One day she arrived with a Swedish-English reader and then I gradually began to make progress. We got along pretty well in a mixture of Norwegian, German, Russian and English with a sprinkling of Chinese and Turki words.

If I have taken Tanya's name for a chapter heading it is because she more than deserves it. As long as I live her name will remain for me a symbol of goodness and kindness.

As I sit here turning the pages of my diary to select a few of the items I scribbled down while I hung in straps in Kuldsha Hospital, I find that there isn't one page on which there isn't something or other written about Tanya. From the time she came to the hospital till I left, not a day passed when she did not do something to gladden or help me.

In appearance she was typically Russian: rather small, but powerfully built and with a round, rather broad face. She was not actually beautiful, but quite pretty, if I can put it that way. She had a wonderfully good smile which was always lurking round her mouth and in her eyes, a smile that was both childish and experienced—enough to make a chap feel like a helpless little boy.

No Moslem was too filthy or evil-smelling for Tanya to smile at as she fussed about him and helped him. I don't know if they have angels in Allah's heaven, but if they do, those fellows must have thought her one of them. Even those inveterate pigs refrained from spitting when she was in the room.

It was no easy task that awaited Tanya Fyodorova in Kuldsha: at eighteen she became the head sister in a hospital with well over a hundred beds, a hospital which was the only one in northern Sinkiang—a part of the world where cleanliness was unknown and disease rampant— and which had a staff that with but few exceptions was as

ignorant and filthy and sluttish as the patients. But it was
not just because of her nice smile and lovely eyes that Tanya
was sent to Kuldsha. She set about the filth and disorder
like a tornado and the Doc rubbed his hands: '*Tanya charasho! Tanya sehr gut!*'

I shall never complain about that last period of my stay
there. Summer was so far advanced that fruits had ripened
and we had apples, cherries and pineapples to eat every
day, and Tanya was always popping in with fresh flowers
till the room was like a greenhouse.

Naturally enough I was rather preoccupied with what
would happen when I was well enough to resume my
travels. And how were Andrew and the others getting on?
When we separated, we had agreed that there was no point
in dividing up our shrunken resources. They left me fifty
Sinkiang dollars and were to telegraph some money to me
as soon as they got in touch with British or Norwegian
authorities. Gradually my dollars had dwindled: a few
extras in the food line and *papyrossos* (cigarettes)—so it
was not surprising that I had begun to get anxious about
that telegram.

Tanya and Elizabeth made inquiries for me at the police-
station and brought back the usual contradictory answers:
Yes, there was a telegram with money for me. No, but I
could expect one in a couple of weeks. Then they were
informed that my companions were waiting for me in
Tihua. Then I discovered that it was no use expecting any
telegram for the simple reason that there was no telegraph
at Kuldsha.

The Doc had told me that I might perhaps hope to get
rid of the sandbag about the middle of July, and then we
would see how my back was doing. I began to count the
days till the middle of the month, as a child does with

Christmas, and I similarly counted the hours till I could
expect a visit from Tanya. Occasionally either she or Maginor would bring me a plate of something that tasted divine,
and I knew that they had cooked it specially for me in their
free time.

However busy Tanya might be, she always found a little
time to spend with me in the evening. There she would sit
on the edge of my bed cutting long strips of gauze, or making something or other that was needed.

Now and again the wondrously beautiful Mira would
swagger in, with a freshly plucked rose in her hair, but
Tanya just snorted contemptuously: '*Mira niet charasho!
Mira niet arbeiten!*'

Then there was one day when little Maginor brought
us a real feast. We had fruit salad and other lovely things,
and then, heavens above, there came a jug of wine and
Russian cigarettes. What could be the meaning of that?
The wine was both good and strong, and before I knew it
I was quite tiddly. A little later in came the Doc along with
a gang of Chinamen, some in uniform, others in elegant
coats. The Doc winked at me, and then Tanya came in and
I heard the explanation: Commissars and other influential
persons from Tihua on inspection.

Afterwards there was a celebration; and when the Sneer
did his round that evening he was as tight as could be,
but cute enough not to say a word. He just stood and
swayed for a moment by each bed. Lussie and Kalanja,
the two nurses who attended him, were also roaring tight.
Kalanja, legs wide apart, steadied herself on the bed of
one of the Moslems and spoke some words of comfort to
the poor wretch. Thereupon both girls slapped their thighs
and roared with laughter. Just at that moment Tanya came
in, and I asked her what Kalanja had said.

'Give the swine seven or eight enemas, then he'll think he's okay.'

But Kalanja failed to hit the door when she followed the Sneer out. She walked straight into the wall and fell back on her behind with a mighty bump.

When I looked closely at Tanya, I could see that she too was very slightly lit.

'What do you think of this hospital?' I asked her. 'Here the nurses drink till they can hardly stand, and even the Sister has one over the eight. I lie writing in my diary and several times on every page I've been writing: *Tanya charasho! Tanya charasho!* Now I suppose I must start writing: *Tanya niet charasho!*'

What queer things women are! For bless me if the girl didn't burst out crying and said that it wasn't much fun being there either and she was only doing her best.

Poor little Tanya! In the end, however, I convinced her that I was just joking and we were friends again.

Wild rumours at the hospital: War in Rumania . . . War in Finland . . . War in Russia. The rumours were flying about for several days before the Doc came and told me that Hitler had begun an attack on Russia.

What was going to happen now? Would the Germans be the victors again? Or would it go the other way, so that I could travel back home across Russia?

It was about this time that Elizabeth and another nurse called Sonya disappeared. I asked Tanya about them, and she told me that unfortunately they had been dismissed because they were German. In reality I expect they had been arrested. I could not help thinking about little Elizabeth: however German she might have been she had done her best. After Tanya she was my best friend in Kuldsha, and I often wonder how she fared and whether she survived the war.

I had now become a bit of a linguist. I had learned the three funny little words it helps such a lot to know in several languages. When it was Mira in the room, I acted the Moslem and said: '*Maesn zahanajata jarritimeun!*' and Mira would stick out her tongue at me. To Li-li with the slanting eyes I was the Chinaman: '*Woh-ei ni!*' and Li-li would clasp her hands and turn her eyes up to heaven. But when I said '*Ja was lubljoo*' to Tanya she just smiled her good smile and blushed all over her face.

One evening when Tanya was sitting with me and we were chatting, she happened to mention that she would be going back to Russia the following year. Almost without thinking, I told her that she could not be too sure about that. Hitler might well take both Moscow and Leningrad and that would be the end of Russia. At that the smile vanished from Tanya's face; she leaped to her feet with blazing eyes:

'*Nie, tovaritch Willie! Hitler Moskau? Nie—Nie!*'

It happened as the Doc had said. In the middle of July I was allowed to get up and try my back. I cut a pretty deplorable figure tottering about on two sticks, and I felt rather despondent when I thought of the long way still ahead of me, whether it were Chungking or the Himalayas.

I had still heard nothing from the others, but the queerest items of information continued to come from the police.

I had been up about a fortnight and things were a tiny bit better, when I received a message from the police to go down there to see them. The Doc arranged for a horse cab and away I went. The police chief received me in person, and to my amazement he informed me that the others were waiting for me in Tihua. I was to take a lorry going there the following day and rejoin them, and to move out of the hospital immediately and spend the last night at the serai.

The Doc shook his head doubtfully when I came back and told him what the police chief had said. He told me that, if I was careful, my back would be all right again in time, or at least I would be free of pain, and there was every chance of its being as good as ever—but go to Tihua by lorry? Well, well . . . he would at least see that I was allowed to sit in the driver's cab.

To be truthful, it was with very mixed feelings that I said goodbye to the Doc, Lulia, Maginor and the others—to say nothing of Tanya. She and I agreed that for that last evening we would go out together to the Asia.

But what on earth was the meaning of the others being in Tihua? It was nearly three months since they had gone from Kuldsha.

And what would it be like having to jolt in a lorry all the way to Tihua with my back?

But at the Asia Tanya and I had steak and onions, a small glass of wine and a glass of vodka. We, who had so often chatted and had fun together and understood each other so well in our weird mongrel language and our gestures and drawings, now sat there and neither of us had a thing to say. And yet perhaps we understood each other just as well as before.

We exchanged presents. Tanya gave me a Russian shirt of fine white linen with blue embroidery down the chest. Curiously enough I had a small thing in my luggage: a little silver chain with a tiny golden pendant. That became Tanya's and she said she would wear it till she died.

'*Spasiba, Tanya . . . Dasvidanja!*'

'*Dasvidanja, tovaritch Willie!*'

Thanks and farewell!

She looked so small and despondent as she walked down the dusty street, back to the hospital, her Moslems, the filth and the flies and the everlasting grind of it all.

With two sticks to help me, stooping and sad at heart, I struggled back to the serai.

7. To General Shun's H.Q.

^^^^^^^^^^^^^^^^^^^^^^^^^^^^^^^^^^^^^

EARLY IN THE morning a policeman came and poked a
filthy finger in my stomach: 'Brrh! Brrh! Automobil. Tihua!'

I managed to work myself into fine spirits. Tihua was
only five hundred or so miles away and in a day or two I
should perhaps meet the others again. Everything would
turn out all right. Besides, Tihua was the actual capital and
there must be a bit more order and sense to be got out of
people where the administration was centralized. Poor fool
that I was! But how was I to know that the more central-
ization you have the more disorder there is?

I don't think I shall ever forget that trip to Tihua even
should I live twice as long as Methuselah.

The policeman and I drove in a horse cab to the police-
station and on the way we passed the hospital. When I saw
Tanya standing there waving a white towel I very nearly
blubbed, and I felt that I wanted to jump out and go back
to hospital all because of her.

At the police-station there was, of course, no lorry, and

I had to sit there waiting in fine Kuldsha-style until far on in the afternoon. The men on duty, however, were quite nice and gave me scalding tea and *papyrossos*. When the lorry did at last come it was a Russian monster, a three-tonner laden with several layers of square, black petrol tins. It was surrounded with a swarm of soldiers armed with revolvers and all sorts of blunderbusses, and the whole horde of them swarmed up on to the tins. Relying on the Doc having reserved me the seat beside the driver, I crawled up into it and sat there. I am perfectly certain that the police were aware of my condition, yet it wasn't long before a soldier came up and tried to pull me out. I shook my head and put a hand on my back:

'*Nie, nie! Balitt pasvonosnik!* (Bad back.)'

But the soldier didn't care a damn about that, and when I protested again he lost his temper:

'*Rotstzasmi!* (Shut your face!)' he sputtered, and I had to give up my seat.

After that I had to start a fresh commotion in order to get the men to understand that I was pretty well crippled and must have help to get up on to the load. Eventually, I got myself squeezed into a place among the clamouring soldiers on top, but when I saw the driver coming, I felt like throwing myself off the lorry again. The yellow oaf who jumped into the driver's seat was none other than the road-hog who had capsized us on my previous attempt to leave Kuldsha. The irons put on him then could not have had any very serious purpose, and obviously it took a good deal in that part of the world before you had your licence taken away.

'If this goes all right, then everything will go all right,' I told myself.

The soldiers were in holiday mood and, as we sped away,

they struck up an appalling chorus which presumably was the Chinese equivalent of *Tipperary*.

Once or twice while I was in hospital I had wondered how I would react to a bit of dangerous driving were I ever let in for it again. Would I be afraid? I don't mind admitting that I was afraid. When that yellow devil of a driver really got going and we drew near the spot where I had got my back broken before, I was as afraid as I have never been either before or since.

Soon, however, there were other things to think about. Some old rag-rugs had been laid over the petrol tins on which we sat, and suddenly I felt that my behind was getting wet. At first I thought that in my fright I had sprung a leak, but then I realized that it was petrol. One of the tins was leaking, and the rags under me and the seat of my trousers were pretty well soaked. The sun was blazing down out of a cloudless sky and if that petrol was like other petrol, what I was sitting on must have been pretty inflammable. The soldiers, however, just went on rolling their *papyrossos*, striking and flicking away burning matches as nonchalantly as though they were drifting on an ice-floe in the Arctic Ocean. That we didn't blow up was an absolute miracle.

My back, however, said no thank you most decidedly to any and every sitting position, and one way or another I just had to lie down. It was a bit of a job getting myself squeezed into a recumbent position among all those legs and guns, but I managed, and so we jolted and bumped away.

Those soldiers realized well enough how things were with me, but not one of them gave me a hand to help me into a more or less tolerable position. On the contrary, it was blatantly obvious that the Turki wit was being largely exercised at my expense. They cracked jokes and laughed and squirted tobacco spit over me from all sides. I don't believe one of them would have worried if they had rattled into Tihua with a dead Anglee. Though of course they wouldn't have carted a corpse along with them for so long, they would just have tipped it out with much shrieking and yelling and left it lying derisively in the ditch. For my part, I prayed to Allah and Buddha and all the demons of the Takla Makan to take them in hand and teach them manners.

The pages in my diary for the days of that trip are blank. Nor was I in the frame of mind to appreciate the beauty or majesty of nature, or whatever is the suitable word for the kind of country through which we drove. But I remember that late in the evening of that first day we were in among mountains and clambering up through a valley. First there were naked sand hills and then wooded slopes, then, farther up, brown parched grass, and farther up still just bare sand and scree. In a pass the driver decided to call it a day, and the soldiers made their arrangements for the night.

I was mighty glad to get my aching shanks down off the lorry, and no sooner down than I stretched myself out on my sleeping-bag—horizontal. It was so warm that there was no point in getting into the sleeping-bag, and food certainly held no interest for me. But the men were hungry and they set about making themselves a *pilav*.

Pilav is always on the menu when you travel in Turkestan, and I had to learn to eat it myself before I was out of Shun do Bahn's fly-ridden republic. It is a dish consisting of rice and mutton—both excellent things in themselves and together—but the pilav the Turkoman likes is so unrea-

The author

Kirghiz child outside a yurt (*The Royal Geographical Society*)

sonably peppered and spiced as to be ruined. The first time I tried it, it felt as though my throat was full of live coals and tacks.

That was my first night beneath the open sky of Turkestan, and it was also the worst. My whole body ached, and there were hundreds of little demons in my back sticking red-hot needles into me. There was no sleep for me, but night brought its myriads of stars and I lay there gazing up at them and thinking my own thoughts and dreaming my own dreams. In a ring round me lay the *élite* of Shun do Bahn's soldiery snoring and blowing like trumpeters.

The cry of some wild animal rang mournfully through the pass and received an answer from far away.

At long last the sun gilded the peaks and heralded in a fresh day on the petrol tins.

All the first day we had been driving north-east. Now having crossed the pass and come down the mountainside we turned due east. The road wound along over plains of sand, and minor passes in smaller mountains. Our speed was automatically reduced, but instead the road took to inclining now to this side, now to that, so that the lorry rolled like a barge in a rough sea. On several occasions we were within an ace of turning over.

It grew hotter and hotter, and in the middle of the day we had to stop for a nap in a little pass. Numerous punctures wasted a lot of time, and we had trouble with the engine too.

When we got a puncture out on the plain the driver had no enviable job lying in the red-hot sand changing wheels, for the heat of the sun shining down on us was nothing compared to the fierce radiation from the ground. Perhaps he thought that the Anglee lying on top of the petrol tins and talking to him in his weird tongue was giving him good advice. But he got no sympathy or hints from me! What I was saying was:

'Serve you right, you yellow devil. And it'll be a good bit warmer in the place where you're going one day. You'll deserve it for doing in Chimpanzee.'

Thus slowly and gradually we trundled eastwards. Now and again we drove through an area of cultivated land, and past a little village surrounded with a thick mud wall. In one place we surprised a flock of antelopes at a spring. Scared by the lorry they galloped off and the soldiers banged away at them with everything they had and every shot missed.

Towards evening we reached a little village surrounded with green fields and orchards. We were to spend another night in the open. The men got hold of a whole heap of melons, and some of them came my way too. The Turkestan sugar melons—*dinje* as the Turkoman calls them—are one of the extenuating circumstances of Sinkiang. If you are in a very good mood and feeling relatively benevolent, you might even go so far as to say that they make up for quite a lot of the filth and general wretchedness of everything else. They are sweet and have a heavenly taste, and quite different to the things we get under the name of melon in Norway. That evening as I lay there gazing northwards across the unending Dsungaria, I did not stop eating till I felt melon almost in my throat. Before I fell asleep, as I did eventually, I saw a silvery two-engined aeroplane fly past heading eastwards. The 'plane from Alma-Ata to some place or other in Asia, I thought. If only I had been in her!

The third day passed without anything special happening —apart from the fact that it became even hotter and my back hurt worse than ever with all the jolting. That evening

I again stuffed myself with melons and slept comparatively well outside another little village.

The following day we started roaring across a great steppe. Soon we came to the river Manas, where it is a couple of miles wide but quite shallow. There was no bridge, but a gigantic tractor of Russian manufacture was to haul us across. The lorry was hitched on with a lot of wires, and off went the tractor into the squelchy mud with us in tow. There were long stretches of just grey surface mud—and it could be a foot or more deep—followed by an islet of dry sand then down into the soup again.

The wheels dug into the miry ground and several times we were within a hair's breadth of capsizing, but 'squelch' it went, and the tractor ploughed on implacably. The old lorry creaked and groaned, and the yells and shrieks of the men were indescribable, but we got across.

We drove out on to the steppe again, and by the time evening came and darkness was falling it was still just flat steppe all around. But the road was gradually growing better and the driver was beginning to make more use of his accelerator. We drove on, and it was nearly midnight when we saw the glow of lights ahead of us.

'Tihua! Tihua!' exclaimed the soldiers excitedly, and even my spirits revived a little. In an hour's time perhaps you will be with the others again, I told myself, and the excitement and anticipation almost made me forget that for four days I had felt much more dead than alive.

For us coming out of the black night of the steppe the lights of Tihua made a fairy-tale sight spread along the hillside. Just before entering the town we saw an aerodrome, glimpsed hangars and 'planes in the darkness, and it all looked so astoundingly civilized. The drive into the town was not unlike that into Kuldsha: there were the same avenues of poplars, the same mud walls and mud houses, but everything was a little more Chinese in character. By the scattered street lamps we could see Chinese inscriptions above doors and on walls, and there were a lot of those roofs like toad stools set on top of one another.

The streets were quiet and empty. Once we were further into the town a herd of emaciated dogs came and kicked up a hullabaloo round the lorry. We came to a long white-washed wall, swung in through a gateway, and stopped in a large rectangular courtyard into which soldiers came swarming to receive us. The long low buildings surrounding the courtyard were all decked with an absolute profusion of red mouldings, flags and stars.

Somehow they got me down off the lorry, some officers swaggered up and gave orders, and a surly soldier with a blunderbuss took up position beside me. The officers and soldiers gradually disappeared through the various doors, and soon there was only the surly creature and I left in the yard. By the houses there was a sentry at almost every door.

It was now after midnight. The moon had risen and was hanging large and yellow over the rim of the wall. Slowly the moonlight spread across the great yard, and one by one the sentries by the doors became transformed into green-painted wooden statues which huddled close in under the walls. On top of the walls was a sentry-walk and small wooden towers with loop-holes like those you see in pictures of medieval castles, and the moon set a thin coating of light on all contours. It was an unreal, fairy-tale atmosphere like a Walt Disney film. As far as I was concerned, swaying there on my feet with exhaustion, the whole thing could have been a dream.

The guard at my side, however, chewed tobacco, grunted a little, spat to right and left, and smelt strongly of Asia.

Even the wooden statues by the doors occasionally turned their heads and sent a jet of tobacco juice out into the yard. And I had a hump of frantic pain on my back; my body felt as heavy as lead and I was so tired that I almost dropped.

No, it was no dream. I was in the capital of Sinkiang, in the H.Q. of Comrade Shun himself. Somewhere, not far away perhaps, were Andrew, Sverre and Atle snoring and asleep.

Nothing happened. I began to wonder if there was trouble brewing.

'*Tovaritch*,' said I to the guard. '*Tri angliski mallsjikki?*'

'*Rotstrasmi!*' he barked and a jet of spittle shot past my face.

'Damned Chink,' said I, and subsided by the side of my rucksack.

Eventually a bouncing, round little officer did appear and barked an order. The guard gave me a kick and I staggered to my feet and followed the officer into one of the houses, the guard at my heels. Inside a large room with white-washed walls, the officer pointed to a stool—and disappeared. I sat down and looked around: a large desk and several stools, some small window-apertures with no glass, and a large picture of the same uniformed brute that the Russian in Shimpanse had on his wall: General Shun in person.

I have no idea how long the guard and I sat staring idiotically at each other before the little officer returned and I was able to fire some questions at him. I tried with '*Tri angliski maltsjikki*' and 'three Norwegian boys', stuck three fingers in the air and indulged in all sorts of pantomime to try and find out something about the others, but the officer hadn't the faintest idea what I was driving at.

He, for his part, blustered and pointed and gestured to all points of the compass, and in the end he too stuck three fingers in the air and said solemnly: '*Nygon, nygon! Serai!*'

Fine! So the lads were in some serai or other here. Even those oafs would understand that I would want to go there too, but the officer just pointed to the big desk, put his hand under his cheek and made some snoring noises that were not to be misunderstood.

All right then, I shall have to wait till the morning. I bowed politely to the officer: '*Spasiba, sjesja!* (Thank you!)' He bowed and withdrew. I laid my sleeping bag on the desk and crawled up onto it. The guard sat himself on a stool by the door with his rifle across his knees and was the very image of a Sinkiang soldier doing his duty.

8. Tihua

WHEN I AWOKE next morning there was a different man on the stool by the door. Nature had not been kind to him. He was uglier than death, the devil and natural sin combined. A red scar running from one corner of his mouth to his temple did not make him any prettier. I was given tea and one or two slices of bread for breakfast. The tea was good, as it is everywhere in that part of the world: weak, but with a good taste. In Kuldsha and Tihua I drank pints of it every day. The Russians call it *tchey*, the Moslems *tch-ay* and in Tihua the Chinese said *Hrasja*.

After an age of waiting the little officer came and made signs to the effect that we were to get going. Out in the courtyard a two-wheeled horse cab awaited us. The vehicle itself was not unlike one of our muck-carts, but on its frame was perched a little house lined with material of a large flower pattern, trimmed with coloured ribbons and cords ending in gorgeous tassels. The horse and its harness were decked out in the same fashion, and the whole affair would have been most suitable in a carnival procession. There were thick curtains across the windows and when the guard and I had seated ourselves inside and the contraption moved off, another curtain was drawn across the door as well.

Once we were out of the gateway I wanted to have a look at things and pulled the curtain away from the window. At that the guard let out a roar, bared his teeth and pulled me roughly away. All I could do was to look sulky and sit on my stool glowering, while we turned corners and rattled along up hill and down dale. Eventually the carriage stopped and we could hear a buzz of voices round us. The guard called out something or other, and after a while a dirty hand was thrust in holding a bit of cloth. This the guard wrapped round my head, took me by the arm and hauled me out.

We walked up some flights of stairs and a door slammed behind us. The cloth was removed from my head and there standing in front of me stood an officer with a mocking smile on his face:

'How do you do?'

All the secrecy, and the loathsome face of that officer standing there sneering so ironically with his squint mouth, combined to make me feel more and more nervous. The first stages of such agitation often make me act with unwonted decision and energy, and so now I grimly mobilized my little English and demanded to be put in immediate touch with my friends.

The brute's smile became more and more mocking. In the end he just stood there laughing at me. I felt my temper rising, and it was no better when he eventually deigned to inform me that the others had left Tihua several months previously. However, I tried to take things more calmly and asked him where they had gone. The supercilious yellow devil was enjoying himself more and more; his slanting eyes almost disappeared in his face with amusement, but for my part I found it very difficult to see anything funny. In the end he told me that they had gone to Kashgar. He embarked on a long rigmarole of which I understood next to nothing, but it was something about me and Kashgar. I lost my temper completely and interrupted to inform him that I had broken my back and could not go to Kashgar and take a stroll across the Himalayas.

'Indeed?' said the swine. 'Is that so?' and his ugly mug became more and more insufferable.

Then, of course, I did something really stupid. With as superior an air as I could muster I demanded to be allowed to send a telegram to the British Legation in Chungking immediately.

If the man had been amused before, he now almost choked with laughter:

'Chungking? Chungking? Hee-hee! Ho-ho!'

Obviously the joke of all time! The officer laughed and laughed, and I became more and more angry. Then, suddenly he changed tactics completely, became grim and serious and pointed to a stool:

'Sit down!'

Slowly it dawned on me that if these chaps thought I was English and perhaps a spy, all that about Chungking was the most idiotic thing I could have said. And when the officer went to the door and called in another, and the two sat down at the table and embarked on a lively discussion, it did not require a genius to know that it was my fate which was being discussed. I was in a sweat of excitement and impatient to know the result.

Then it occurred to me that perhaps it would improve

my position if I could get the misunderstanding cleared up and stop them thinking I was English. So up I hopped:

'No English . . . Norwegian!'

Both looked inquiringly at me and at each other, then they shook their heads. I tried again:

'Yes, Norwegian. Scandinavian. Fridtjof Nansen. Roald Amundsen!'

They were none the wiser and the one with the smile motioned to me to sit down on the stool again. But I wasn't intending to give up so easily:

'Yes, Norwegian! Oslo! Quisling!'

That went home. That was a sound they recognized. The smile disappeared from the yellow face of the laughy one. His squint mouth became a thin line and his eyes were cold as he walked across and stood in front of me, legs wide apart:

'No English?'

'No, no!'

'German?'

He rapped the question out like the crack of a whip, and in a flash I realized I had again made a first-class bloomer. If it was not good that they should think me English, there would be all hell to pay if they took me for a German. Their great models—the Russians—were fighting for their lives against the Germans, and Comrade Shun's officers were not so thick-headed that they did not know all about it. There was nothing for it but to deny poor old Norway her independence.

'No, no! No German! From Norway in England!'

Then I twirled about the floor trying to make them understand that I was on my way to Canada to learn to fly so that I could do in as many of the damned Germans as possible. I flapped my arms and shouted: 'Rat-tat-tat—boom,

boom!' I drew my hand across my throat and said: 'All Germans—so!' Then the two of them laughed till they shook, and the situation was saved for the time being. As soon as they had recovered, they resumed their discussion. On and on they talked, but finally they appeared to have reached agreement.

'Okay,' said the smiling one. The telegram to Chungking should go. Meanwhile I should be taken to a serai and could take things easy there.

The guard received his orders, and he and I got into another horse cab. This time there were no curtains across the windows, nor were my eyes bandaged. The cab rattled off into the town and it was not long before we reached the serai—a large and impressive specimen of its kind. We drove through a gateway into a covered courtyard. On the two long sides there were verandas running round the ground and first floors and long rows of doors leading into the rooms. The verandas had slender balustrades painted in every sort of gorgeous colour. By the mud wall, bang opposite the gateway, was a faithful copy of the 'toilet' in Kuldsha's famous serai. One refinement, however, there was: the roof instead of being flat was built on poles in a very complicated structure, and all along the eaves were open loop-holes. Some loose shutters lying there were obviously used to close the holes during the winter.

My guard conferred with a Chinaman and I was conducted up to a room on the first floor. It was a rectangular hutch, roughly six feet by six feet. Along one side was a low mud-bunk. By the door on to the veranda was a tiny opening for a window. Walls, floor and ceiling, of course, all made of mud. It was much more like a cell than anything else, and that impression was enhanced when the guard drew the mighty bolt on the outside of the door.

The entire establishment could easily have been taken for a prison, for the only windows were those tiny peep-holes on to the verandas.

Nonetheless it was a serai, not a prison. You could see that when you took a look at the people sitting on the veranda taking their ease. A little to the left of my room sat a Chinaman in a black silk housecoat eating rice with chopsticks. The lacquered shoes on his small feet were among the most splendid I had so far seen in Turkestan. Nonetheless he looked an absolute pauper compared with the mountain of Moslem flesh I had on my right, dressed in white and incredibly wide silk breeches stuffed into beautifully polished high boots. The light sparkled on the great pendants that dangled from his ears, and his fat fingers were covered with sparkling rings. His moustache was waxed and glossy and black and fine. The Corsair in person.

My guard put up a camp bed outside my door. Even though I had landed in the best serai in Tihua it was impossible to help feeling a prisoner. I just had to take things calmly. Wait and see!

When I got to know my guard of more-than-horrible-appearance a little better, I discovered that he was both a decent chap and straight. He spoke a little Russian, which was just about as intelligible as mine, and in time we became quite friendly. His nasty scar was a memento from a scrap outside Canton when he was doing his bit in the war with the Japanese. His name was Yh-Shyn-San, or something like that, but I think it will be simpler just to call him Canton.

He was not an unreasonable man, and taking it all in all I had quite a tolerable time while I was in his charge.

When I wanted to go to the 'installation', I banged on the door and Canton went down with me and stood there stiffly at attention, patiently waiting with his triangular bayonet until I had finished.

Once a day he took me out into the town to eat. When the time came, he opened the door and off we shuffled to a Russian restaurant which was incredibly dirty even for the capital of Sinkiang. Flies were all over it in their usual myriads, but the food was fine. They served both Russian and Chinese dishes, but I stuck consistently to the Russian.

On our way home Canton always liked to go into a shop to buy something for the day's other meals. He might buy wheaten bread, rice, or melons. Now and again he did a deal with one of the screeching sellers of Indian corn who walked about crying their wares with an appalling clamour of howls and screeches. One of these was a daily visitor to the courtyard of the serai. It was quite a sight to watch the little, emaciated, humpbacked Chinaman come shuffling in with his two large baskets of maize which he carried slung from a pole across his shoulder. The baskets swung this way and that as he walked, and the old boy had to ply his legs as hard as he could to avoid going head over heels.

On our way to and from the restaurant we attracted a considerable amount of attention. Everybody turned round to stare at us, some spat at me, but I soon learned to cock my head in the air and give them a scornful look in exchange.

I didn't manage to see much more of Tihua than what lay along our route from the serai to the restaurant, but it was enough to enable me to discover a certain difference between that town and Kuldsha. Even though there were plenty of the ordinary mud houses with flat roofs, there were also many with terraced roofs. In the streets too there were many more slanting-eyed, little, yellow people, even though the Chinese were still definitely in the minority compared with the Moslems. Here and there you could see a house which was both elegant and imposing, with large ponds and plantations round it, but, as in Kuldsha, the little temples took first prize. What a striking contrast there was between those lovely, well-designed temples with green patches round them and ringed with a white-washed wall, and the shabby and generally dilapidated appearance of the rest of the town.

One week passed and there hadn't been a squeak out of the H.Q. I still had a lot of Oriental patience to acquire and I roused Canton into going up to the H.Q. with me to see if we could find out anything. Naturally I was given the usual answers:

'Telegram from Chungking? Coming tomorrow—perhaps in three months . . . the telegraph's not working this week. Take it calmly—wait and see.'

Little by little Canton became quite amenable. Occasionally he would let me sit on the veranda; now and again he would accept a cigarette and we would sit there and chat, a little falteringly I must admit, but it was pleasant nonetheless.

Quite near to the serai was a large house which I imagine was the largest in Tihua. It's not often you see so many red mouldings, stars and flags all in one place. The most sensational thing about it, however, was some huge placards like cinema posters stuck on the walls. As a joke I asked Canton if we couldn't go to the cinema, and he at once said that he would ask his chiefs. Off we strode to the H.Q. and to my amazement permission was given at once.

Canton very proudly showed me round the exterior premises before we went into the hall itself. It was obviously a sort of Party House, for there were rooms with bookshelves, maps on the walls and plenty of pictures of Lenin, Stalin and Comrade Shun. A whole gang of young boys were very busy in there, and they all had red stars on their caps.

The cinema hall had an earthen floor that was inclined just as in a proper cinema. There were some benches right up in front and on the foremost of these officers were seated. Behind them were some relatively well-dressed civilians, and then some of the young hopefuls with stars on their caps. In the standing room behind the benches was the usual mixture of Chinamen and Moslems of every kind. And right at the back Canton and myself.

As usual my presence attracted a flattering amount of attention. They all stared at me as though I were some rare animal. All chewed tobacco and spat unconcernedly. The stench was concentrated Sinkiang.

The small films at the beginning showed parades in Moscow, and there was Comrade Joseph showing people his lovely smile. Applause broke out at the first glimpse of his moustache; the audience clapped and cheered like mad. The main film was about flying and that fascinated them. However, it is one thing to speak a few words of Russian and another to follow the dialogue in a film. I am afraid the propaganda was wasted as far as I was concerned.

One day I paid a visit to the barber for a haircut. While this was being seen to, Canton stood waiting as usual with fixed bayonet. The shop did not lack a certain elegance.

It was open to the life of the street, of course, but the other three walls had once in the remote past been papered and now they were almost entirely covered with pictures of the three great ones. A cracked piece of glass on the wall bore distant traces of once having had a mercury backing, and on a shelf were a couple of bottles of hair oil marked 'Moscow'. In one corner was a wash basin—what on earth would that be used for?

The owner was a well-bred person who did not spit on the floor, but directed his regular jets of tobacco juice at the basin in the corner. That he usually missed was of no importance.

It was a painful procedure getting rid of my beautiful week-old beard, and, that done, I had to call upon Canton to help me save some of the hair on my head.

Three weeks passed and still I had idiotic replies to my inquiries at the H.Q. 'Come again next week'. 'Wait and see'.

The heat grew worse and worse and in the end was almost intolerable. I spent most of the time lying on my bunk gasping for air like a fish out of water. I was growing more and more fearful that I would never get away from Tihua at all, and eventually I was afraid the intolerable heat would make me quite imbecile.

One day as I lay sweating on my bunk I suddenly found myself back on the platform saying goodbye to my parents: there were the mountains, their ridges like white knife-edges against the night-blue winter sky, there the Pole Star and Charles's Wain, all the sparkle of the stars and the whole picture was distinct and so pure—like a jewel of silver and blue enamel. I realized then that I must do something to get away from Tihua. All at once I knew what: the Russians! Perhaps the Russians would fix it for me.

I fished paper and pencil out of my rucksack, and the Swedish-English reader Tanya had given me. Laboriously I concocted the sentences I felt the situation required. Then I thundered on the door for Canton and told him I wanted to go to the H.Q. To myself I swore a mighty oath that now little Willie was going to get away from Tihua or else get himself into a real prison.

As it happened it was my laughing friend of the first interview who received me. First I told him that I wished to know what had happened about the telegram to Chungking. At once his loathsome mocking smile appeared and, after a little beating about the bush, he explained that unfortunately they had no telegraph, and that they had, in any case, no link with Chungking. Therefore I could safely return to the serai and get back to sleep.

I felt rage oozing out of every part of my body, and I told him that telegraph or no telegraph I now wanted to get away from Tihua.

'Indeed? Very interesting! And where do you wish to go to?'

Slowly and haughtily I played my trump card:

'Will you kindly be good enough to put me in touch with the Russian Consul at once. I have very good connections in Moscow.'

The sarcastic smile vanished. In a moment he had become a different and much nicer man.

'Of course, of course. But most regrettably the Russian Consul is not here today. But come back tomorrow and we'll arrange it for you.'

Strangely enough he did arrange something. Even though the following day the Russian was still regrettably

absent from Tihua, yet it appeared that there was a car
leaving for Kashgar the very next day and, if I wished to
go with it, I should be welcome to do so.

So it was to be Kashgar and the Himalayas after all.
By that time I would gladly have turned my steps in any
direction as long as it led away from Tihua.

The following day we started out on a memorable tour
round Takla Makan.

9. *The Silk Road*

ΛΛΛΛΛΛΛΛΛΛΛΛΛΛΛΛΛΛΛΛΛΛΛΛΛΛΛΛΛΛΛ

THE NEXT MORNING Canton and I got to the headquarters early but as yet there was no sign of any car.
Though every man and beast at the headquarters seemed
busily engaged getting the expedition under way, it was
nearly nine o'clock in the evening before we were ready to
start.

Again the conveyance was a lorry and its load the usual
rectangular petrol tins. Over these an awning had been
rigged on a makeshift framework and beneath it the
passengers were stowed. It was rather a squeeze to get us
all on, for as well as a gang of soldiers and myself, there
was a civilian Chinese couple, the officer in charge of the
expedition and his pretty little wife.

Our commander was a plump and jovial chap in the
usual uniform covered with Sinkiang stars and a lot of
other frippery. Like all the other officers he was a Chinaman, but he was obviously of mixed blood. Thick black
eyebrows above his slanting eyes gave him a peculiar

appearance. He smiled almost as persistently and cosily as had Chimpanzee and he smoked cigarettes uninterruptedly. Taken by and large, he was a decent, gentlemanly chap. He glowed with pride at the task entrusted to him, and there are no words for the expression on his face as he placed my papers in a yellow leather briefcase which, from then on, he never let out of his sight.

His little yellow wife was an absolute revelation of Chinese beauty and charm. From her tiny feet to her well-groomed hair, which had the appearance of wood shavings lacquered black, she was the typical Chinese woman. Her clothes, however, were fairly European, though hardly the most suitable garments for a trip in a lorry across a sandy desert. She always wore an ankle-length dress, and each morning she fished yet another one out of her baggage. Much as she adored variation in colour her dresses all had two things in common: all were of silk and all clung as tightly to her neat plump figure as a snake's skin. One could hardly have wanted a more charming travelling companion.

Both husband and wife glittered with a profusion of gold fillings in their teeth. That may just have been their method of storing the family fortune; if not, it can only have been a form of ostentation, for their teeth were so white and looked so sound that it was impossible to believe that they could ever have had so many holes in them.

We had two drivers who were to drive in shifts, and these motor-minded sons of the East—more proud of their knowledge than any professor awarded a Nobel Prize—naturally appropriated the two seats in the cab with the result that the officer's wife and the other Chinese woman had to squeeze in along with the rest of us on top of the load.

The only thing to detract from my joy at finally leaving the glorious capital of Sinkiang was a slight sense of disappointment at not having had a glimpse of the redoubtable Comrade Shun.

When at long last we did get under way we dashed along across plains and sand dunes, and then began climbing up a mountain valley. In Sinkiang there are two tree lines, an upper and a lower. This is because in the lower-lying parts it is too dry for trees to live. Up in the mountains, however, there is a good rainfall, and there both deciduous trees and conifers grow strongly until you reach so high that ice and snow put an end to all life.

We jolted along until three o'clock that night, by which time we were fairly high up in the mountains. There we rested for three hours, before piling back on the lorry. Then, having negotiated a pass, we began descending the southern slopes of the mountain in long curves.

Kashgar lay somewhere far to the south-west. That much I did know. But the whole time we were heading south-east, perhaps mostly east, and I began to wonder whether I was not perhaps being 'taken for a ride'. I questioned the officer:

'No Kashgar?—*Niet Kashgar?*' I asked.

'*Oh-ri, oh-ri Kashgar jaksee! Da, da, Kashgar charasho!* Yes, yes, Kashgar, okay.'

That was all right. Shun do Bahn's trusted officer was a linguist, and with occasional recourse to sign language, there was no difficulty in getting a conversation going. He was in fact most forthcoming and explained that I had no need to worry—to Kashgar I should go—but first we must go through the Turfan oasis.

The oasis and town of Turfan lie due south of the great mountain Bogdo Ola. Mountains lie in a semicircle round the town to the north, but to the south there is just the desert. The lowest part of this desert lies more than 650 feet below sea level, and, warm as it had been in Tihua, that was nothing to what it was in Turfan—like hell itself.

A fine and fertile oasis surrounded the town: there were orchards, vegetable plots and fields of rice and maize. The water for the town and the cultivated area runs in conduits which are for the most part underground—thanks to the labour of earlier generations—and today the people of Turfan obtain their daily bread without having to exert themselves to any great degree. The presence of water and the forcing heat do most of the work. If the people of Turfan are lazy, one can hardly blame them. Who would not become lazy living in such a furnace?

We drove along between fruit trees and patches of vegetables, and then came to a little gateway in a huge mud wall through which the lorry just managed to squeeze. It was obvious at once that the dwellings in Turfan broke all records for dilapidation and primitiveness. But even though a large proportion of the town's population was still pretty near the troglodyte stage, Comrade Shun had already been there with his red paint and smartened things up a bit.

As we hooted through the clusters of Moslems on our way to the bazaar we passed a *tsai-chana* (tea-house), its two storeys making it tower up out of the wretched drabness. Neither first nor second storey boasted a wall on the street side. The curtainings for the various compartments were rolled up on poles and you could look right in and see the Moslems squatting on their hams on the earthen floors enjoying their *tsai* or pilav. Walls, floors and roof were made of the usual mixture of mud, straw and dung with here and there the end of a poplar branch protruding.

Every floor and every wall sagged in one direction or another, and you felt disaster was imminent, that in another moment the Moslems on the second floor must tumble right upon the lousy pates of those below.

In Turfan for the first time I saw a covered bazaar. Whole streets were covered with rush mats laid on a framework of poplar branches. Here and there would be a little opening that admitted a strip of light. There, in the middle of the day, while the sunshine poured down over Turfan out of a cloudless sky, you could walk in gloomy twilight. Among the indescribably colourful clusters of Moslems in front of the ramshackle dwellings a European could imbibe as much of the mystery of the East as he could possibly wish, to say nothing of all the Oriental scents and smells he would also inhale!

The expedition paid a courtesy visit to the police-station; the Anglee they had with them was well scrutinized by both high and low, but up on top of the petrol tins he was safe—no inhabitant of Turfan had the energy to spit so far. On the one occasion when he came down off the load and entered a *tsai-chana* to get something to keep body and soul together, he was guarded by the golden teeth of the officer and his wife gleaming on either side of him.

However, we had to be on our way to Kashgar. We must wave farewell to the people of Turfan, and, while the sweat trickled from every pore in our bodies, we drove on westward across a glowing desert to the oasis of Taksun and the town of that name.

Taksun is something of a large town. It has impressive military barracks and other things as well. My diary records one remarkable occurrence: 'In a *tsai-chana* I had the pleasant surprise of getting a little water in a proper wash basin and so was able to scrub off the worst of the dirt.'

And I imagine that my performance with a tooth-brush long remained a subject of eager discussion. In Sinkiang you have to brush your teeth with tea—the first and most necessary lesson one learns east of Shimpanse is never to let water that has not been boiled pass your lips.

It is not much use searching the encyclopaedias and reference books for information about the population of Sinkiang. Some give it as a million and a half, others say that it is four to five million. In Kuldsha I was told it was six million. No one will expect me to know the correct answer, but I am at least sure that a million and a half is too low. At any rate something must be wrong when reputable English and German maps mark Kuldsha, Taksun and Aksu as being tiny little places in comparison with Kashgar and Tihua. My impression certainly was that Kuldsha and Aksu were quite as populous as Tihua and almost as large as Kashgar. Taksun was not so very far behind them either. Perhaps the reason is that Kashgar is the town best known to Europeans, and Tihua the capital.

After jolting across another desert west of Taksun, we once more came up among high and savage mountain passes. These passes could occasionally furnish a surprise: just as you were driving along in country where all was stone and naked rock and grey-brown sand, you would round a spur and, hey presto! there you were in a little paradise of a valley with a river gambolling along its floor —a place of green slopes and woods. In one such valley, where people had settled with their beasts, I saw houses that had been built of stones.

Mostly it was sterile, sandy desert and naked rock. Wonderfully beautiful it often was nonetheless, even where the landscape was as desolate as death. Seldom have I seen such splendour of colour as in the evenings on the southern slopes of the Celestial Mountains (Tien Shan), when the different strata in the mountainsides shone and glittered in a sunset.

Day after day, with much changing of gear, backing and cutting, the two drivers brought us nearer and nearer to Kashgar.

When a crowd of people sit huddled on a layer of petrol tins, are jostled and shaken together for several days on end, a certain metamorphosis occurs: the dust, sweat and fumes become, so to speak, common property; bodies, arms and legs gradually run into an almost homogenous mass, which in its turn becomes more and more one with the load and the lorry, reacting in the same way and at the same time to its swaying, lurching movements.

When the wheels on one side dig down into the sand and the lorry threatens to capsize, when the driver sweating and cursing, changing gear and accelerating, finally manages to get the lorry running more or less level again and it immediately heels over at a threatening angle to the other side—then the lump of humanity on top follows the movements like a rider does those of his horse and similarly tries to help the poor brute.

It was a strange road, and a strange name it had: the Silk Road. It was certainly not because it was smooth that it was given the name, but because silk was the most important commodity carried by the caravans that have used it since the olden days. Across the sand dunes there is, in many places, no road as such at all. The desert wind has obliterated the tracks of centuries of camel traffic, and even up on the mountain passes it was only at the worst places that any attempt at levelling had been made. Rivers were crossed sometimes on bridges that restored one's belief that the age of miracles was not past, and sometimes the lorry had to become amphibian. There was the excitement of never knowing whether it would not tumble both us and its load into dirty, muddy soup. But then, of course, it is not a road that was built by engineers with levelling instruments and all the rest of their paraphernalia, but one that has been trodden and trampled by camels, horses, donkeys and human beings in a thousand years of movement from east to west and from west to east.

Lying there on a lurching lorry it was easy to picture to oneself how man has made his way along that road since time immemorial. Long before history had anything to tell, the stars showed the way. Afterwards, the hordes of Ghenghis Khan thundered past on horseback. In recent days, perhaps Sven Hedin and his people came that way, their eyes skinned for desert cities that man had abandoned or the wind buried. Christian missionaries have toiled along it in the vain hope of wresting a precious soul or two from Allah.

Many brave toilers lie along it. It is the last resting place of many a camel, horse and donkey that has succumbed to the hardships. Many a weatherbeaten Mongolian and slant-eyed Chinaman have here sighed out their last breath. Of the odiferous true believers of Turkestan there are many who have here stroked their beards for the last time. Pale skeletons along the road bear witness to all that. Out in the desert, up on the passes and in the narrow valleys —everywhere lie skeletons and skulls, grinning. Skeletons large and small, piles of bones and solitary femurs. Horse? Camel? Man? It is not easy to decide as you rattle past . . .

On this occasion, however, it was a young Norwegian who sat squeezed between soldiers on a lurching lorry and with receptive senses took in sights and impressions so

strange and wonderful that they made him forget the
fatigue of his body and the pain in his back.

Through deserts, in among mountains, across passes,
down into valleys and out into desert again . . . thus it
was the whole way from Tihua to Kashgar. The route
creeps along on the southern side of the Celestial Mountains
in a wide arc round Takla Makan, the Wilderness of Death.

Down from the mountains, rivers, large and small, flow
out into the desert sand and disappear: the Aksu Daria
from the Tien Shan, the Kashgar Daria from the Trans
Altai, the Yarkand Daria from Mount Goodwin Austen
in the Karakorum, and the Khota Daria from the Kwen-
lun are some of them that manage to reach so far that
together they form the river Tarim, which makes every
effort to achieve a junction with the Tiertsen Daria from
the eastern Kwen-lun and the Kontshe Daria from the
Kuruk Mountains—but in vain. Implacable, the Takla
Makan exhausts and destroys them all.

Each time a geographic expedition has been in this
strange desert, the map has had to be altered. Rivers and
lakes are always drying up and shrinking, and vegetation
has to keep closer and closer to the mountains in order to
live.

All the oasis towns that we passed on our crooked way
to Kashgar lay either on or near a river that came from
the Tien Shan. There was a whole collection of them:
Yentiky, Karashar, Charchi and Bugur, Chulabad, Kutsha,
Saram, Bai and Aksu. The one oasis was lovelier than the
other, the one town more weird than the next—and each
day more confusedly full of impressions than the others.

And if the days were wonderful, the nights were no less
so.

Once we had trouble with the lorry out in the sandy

desert. Evening came. We sat there groaning and watched
the sun drown in a blood-red lake away out in the sand
ahead of us where the heat haze was like a purple wall
around it. Sleep? No, not where gusts of hot air came off
the sand with such force that you felt you could sail away
on them. Sweat ran down us in streams, and the sand was
burning hot to the touch.

Some nights we spent shivering in the mist under a
precipitous mountain wall up on a pass, with a roaring
mountain torrent to lull us to sleep. Other nights we spent
sleeping sweetly on a mud bank in a caravanserai in one
of the towns, while nose and lungs most reluctantly inhaled
the rank smell of Moslem.

Marco Polo said of the Takla Makan that it was so long
that it took a year to ride from one end to the other, and
it took a month to cross it at its narrowest point. He told
how the caravans made their way from one watering-
place to the next and how the leaders of the caravans
'dressed' the camels in a straight line and sighted along
this line to keep their course. When in the evening they
halted at an oasis, they set up stakes to show the direction
for the next day's march before lying down to sleep. He
tells of poisonous grass and of poisonous water at individual
oases, and of the peculiar sounds which the traveller will
hear if he is so unlucky as to get separated from the
caravan: bells and musical instruments, drums, the beat
of hooves, the sound of men talking. Such things he will
hear right out in the desert, and should he follow these
sounds, then Death and Takla Makan are sure to have
him—for it is with those noises that the demons of the
desert fool people and lure them in whence none returns
alive.

However, we heard none of that devil's music, nor did

it look as though our drivers had any difficulty with the direction.

Now and again we met a camel caravan: in long rows the great brutes shuffled past, legs moving in loose-jointed ungainliness. From the wooden pin stuck in the nose of each hung the rope that tied it to the saddle of the one in front. They swayed along with heavy bales of merchandise on their backs. On one or another sat a Moslem in deep and contemplative meditation—the perfect illustration of the fact that here there was no haste. The little camel bells rang with the same sound as in the days of Marco Polo.

It would be too much of a rigmarole to take each day of that trip through the deserts and across the mountain passes, and to describe each one of the towns through which we passed. Let me rather describe a typical day.

The desert road, along which we bumped and jolted was in places a fairly hard-trodden and smooth strip of anything up to several yards wide; elsewhere it was wind-blown and hidden beneath a fine layer of sand. Round us were ridges of sand, gently sloping, low and uniform. The lines in the mountain landscape could remind you of the eastern parts of Norway if in imagination you could shave the Norwegian mountains of their soil and trees and have the whole sprinkled with a layer of sand several feet thick. There was the usual heat haze full of dust to restrict our field of vision across the dunes that encompassed us in all directions.

Suddenly the horizon ahead of us darkened and we found ourselves driving straight towards an ochre-coloured cloud that came sweeping across the country. The *harmsil*, that blistering desert wind that whips up the fine sand-dust and sends it swirling in clouds, was advancing upon us.

The Chinese officer's charming little wife wrapped her pretty head in shawls; the soldiers took similar precautions, and I followed their example as best I could.

Then the *harmsil* was upon us and in an instant the pulverized sand-dust had settled like a bright yellowy-grey snow-fall over everything and everybody, and had covered us with a thick layer. It penetrated our wrappings, mixed with our perspiration and lay greasy, sticky and nasty, over our faces. Luckily, that was a relatively innocuous type of *harmsil* which did not last long, and soon we saw ahead of us a mountain with a cleft in it: another pass for us to cross.

As we climbed up the mountain towards that pass, the sand grew coarser and coarser and became mixed with stones; then it was all stone, and in the end there was just the naked mountain. Tall boulders protruded here and there; at a distance they resembled gigantic cairns, but when you came closer they were just weathered blocks of sandstone.

We crossed the pass, zigzagged down on the other side and set off over a fresh stretch of desert.

Towards evening something bright and silvery and green began shimmering beyond the reddish yellow desert. That, we knew, meant an oasis. Soon a lone tamarisk bush appeared, then before we knew it, we were driving down an alleyway of poplars with golden cornfields bellying out on either side. We passed scattered mud huts and small clusters of adobe houses surrounded by a grey wall. Apples, pineapples, and grapes glowed invitingly from green trees. Grey muddy water gurgled in dykes and conduits. We began meeting bare-legged, jacketed Moslems. Shock-headed women and half-naked children goggled after us in amazement. In one place the road was bounded by a long wall over which we could see, and inside a great party was being held in a lushly fertile garden. On a most colourful carpet spread on the grass beneath some trees sat a number of people on their hunkers apparently having a lovely time.

Though not yet in the town, we could see its wall winding like a snake as it followed the gentle contours of the ground. Here and there the snake acquired a hump in the guise of a tower; a gateway was like a dark patch on its belly and up its side. Between us and this dark patch lay the oasis' burial ground, the *guristan* of the Moslems. The graves were like anthills, rows of them on terrace-like slopes built facing the town wall: a tamarisk, a solitary poplar, and here and there something that might have been taken for a monument or a mausoleum.

There, then, reposed the earthly trappings of the sons and daughters of the oasis who had passed on, but not under the six feet of soil that we pile on top of our tired limbs. The Moslems believe that the soul has a fixed, definite number of days at its disposal in which to leave the dead body, and therefore the corpse is laid in a chamber built of earth and provided with an opening through which the soul can get out. Unfortunately it can happen that while the soul is busy crawling out, dogs and rats and other animals get in and help themselves to what the soul has relinquished. Sometimes they drag a piece of this or that outside, so that there are a lot of curious things to be seen lying about these *guristans*.

The road skirted the edge of the burial-ground, the lowest terrace of which had collapsed where it faced the road, and the roadside was now littered with bones and lumps of soil. The front wheels sent a grinning skull spinning, and in the wheel track behind us I saw part of a thigh bone that had been driven down into the ground.

It was touch and go, but our make-shift awning came un-scathed through the gateway and there we were inside the town. The groups of argumentative Moslems that clustered in the street must willy-nilly make way for the lorry and its soldiers. We turned and twisted along the narrow streets and alleys and stopped at a long low house with two wings. We had found our serai for the night.

The serai was bustling with life. In the back courtyard was parked the queerest collection of Turkoman vehicles; brown melancholy camels stood tethered to the posts from their nose-pegs, horses whinnied and donkeys brayed.

'*Hosh! Hosh!* (Goodbye! Goodbye!) *Drostee honseema!* (Good day!) *Pannika, pannika!* (Au revoir!) *Kaider be-lasee! Kaider barasee!* (Whence do you come? Whither are you going?)' The Turkoman syllables buzzed round our ears. If you judged by such a serai, you would think that they must be the world's most itinerant people.

Among themselves they were very sociable; there was endless stroking of beards, clapping of backs and kissing of cheeks, but there was nothing to indicate that anyone was glad to see my uniformed guides. Quite the contrary. And what the Moslems thought of my own humble person was unfortunately never in doubt. I was a bandit. A *parang*. Son of a damned infidel dog of an Anglee . . . and you spat after him! As we passed, the usual comment was: '*Kishak parang!*' which perhaps can be most decently trans-lated as 'filthy foreigner'.

I have seen the Turkomans described as a courteous people. That may be so if you come travelling with ser-vants and baggage and the best of equipment, as the great personage, the sahib. I can well imagine them being polite then. But when you are alone and a foreigner and in charge of the police or soldiers, then the Turkomans have not

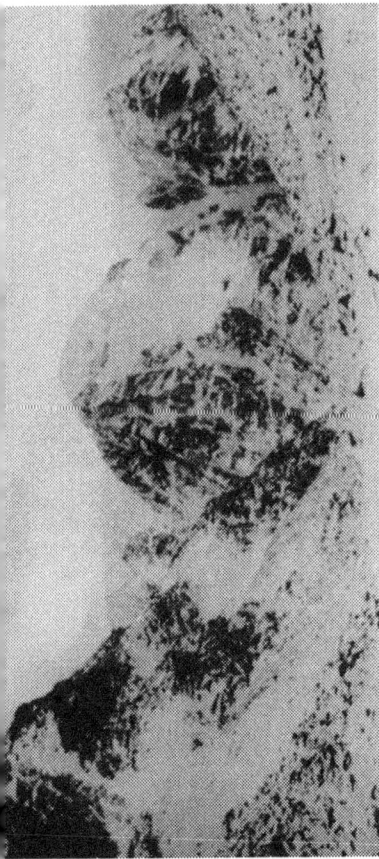

On the Roof of the World—Mintaka Pass
(*M. C. Gillett*)

Tasj Kurghan and the Sarikol Valley (*Sir Clarmont
P. Skrine*)

The British Consulate at Kashgar
Clarmont P. Skrine)

A caravan climbing up the Chichiklik
Pass (*Sir Clarmont P. Skrine*)

much courtesy to lavish on you. That at least was my experience. Anyway, it was sufficient to be in the clutches of the police for people to spit after you, however much of a true believer you might have been. I saw several examples of that.

There were other things that I found difficult to reconcile with what I saw. For example, I had been told that the orthodox Moslem may not smoke tobacco or drink alcohol. If that is true, then Allah's grip on souls in the oases of Turkestan is very loose indeed. There was a *papyrosso* hanging from every man's mouth, and I saw several who were well under the weather. Perhaps the new times are ruining people's morals there too.

The farther we came from Tihua, the smaller was the Chinese element in the population, and in the end it was hardly noticeable at all. I began to notice a special type of Moslem that was very numerous: people with aquiline noses and pronouncedly bow-shaped mouths. Many of them were quite light in the skin and really handsome. The women at times had black horsehair veils in front of their faces.

Another thing you could not help noticing was the appalling prevalence of goitre. I should imagine that some fifty per cent of the people were marked by this disease.

As we sat on top of the load of tins and jolted and swayed on and on along the road to Kashgar it was possible even to grow bored. That at least is how the lovely little wife of the officer, who sat slightly in front of me, must have been feeling one day. That day the dress she was wearing had a coquettish slit up the side that reached some way above her knee, and certainly no one could have taught that little lady with the slanting disingenuous eyes how to make better use of it by showing to us all that her legs were superb all the way up. Black silk and thoroughly decent knickers underneath, of course, but all the same. . .

As I sat there I began to wonder whether I had looked so deeply into those slanting eyes that I had become cockeyed myself, or was it that the frivolous little creature was really trying to start a flirtation behind the very back of her honourable spouse? But, yes, she brought up all her guns, big and little: winking and smiling and running the tip of her tongue along her lips—and no one shall tell me that that was the first time she had made a frontal attack!

What on earth does one do in such a situation?

On the one hand there was no doubt that if I had responded it might have been very risky. Though I had seldom, if ever, met a man who appeared more good-natured than that star-spangled husband of hers, yet that was hardly sufficient to justify one assuming that he would tolerate anything. Suppose he turned fierce, stuck out his chest and brandished that great pistol of his? And, perhaps, challenged me to a duel behind the latrine of the serai where we were to spend the night? After that, it might well have been my bones that would have come under the lorry's wheel next time a European drove that way.

On the other hand, she *was* an unusually luscious little piece, and it would be rather ignominious not to react at all. Yet, taking it all in all, it was perhaps best to keep on the safe side.

The little cherry-blossom was obviously disappointed. She must have considered the Anglee an appallingly dumb and boring fish. After stopping the glad eye, she made a remark about me—which of course I did not understand. The others understood all right! There was no doubt of

that, for it set them off in the coarsest of laughter I have
ever heard. It must have been a remarkably witty jest,
for they all crowed and laughed till I thought they would
tumble off into the desert sand.

I, the object of it all, was quite out of the picture. However, I gave the little beauty a long and languishing look,
said demonstratively 'ha-ha' and 'hee-hee' and told her, in
Norwegian, that I did not consider it anything to laugh
about: 'Do you understand that, you silly little dolled up
Chinese chit?'

From Tihua to Kashgar was what I call my vegetarian
period, for I ate nothing but fruit and vegetables—especially an infinity of melons. The melons of Turkestan have
most excellent qualities, as I have described before, but
if they assume too dominant a position in one's diet, they
are apt to display other and less desirable characteristics.
After the initial sweet encounter with palate and stomach
some of their components develop an irresistible longing
for mother earth, become expansive, if not explosive . . .

After one long day in the desert we reached our serai
in the evening, just at the moment when my loathsome
inside decided that now it would . . . I got behind the
local hoarding, but only just in the nick of time.

It is not easy to say which of the oasis towns we passed
through was the most lovely and wonderful. I believe,
though, that I would give my vote to Aksu. I should think
in the Aksu oasis we drove through a continuous area of
cultivated land that was a good fifty miles in extent.

There are really two towns of Aksu, an old and a new;
or perhaps they had better be called the Moslem and the
Chinese. They lie about three miles apart, and both are
surrounded by a picturesque wall that winds hither and

thither and has romantic gateways and towers. Each has a *guristan* with plenty of forefathers' bones strewn about it.

Here, as nowhere else, you can lose yourself in picturesque alleyways of ramshackle huts and hovels. In the variegated hurly-burly of the bazaar you are captivated by the East, as nowhere else. The swarms of flies are denser, the smell of Moslem more concentrated and ranker than anywhere else. But, on the other hand, there are not many places where the temples are more wonderful or the gardens of the rich Moslems more beautiful.

Aksu and the surrounding district can also stand as an example of the fabulous fertility of the oases of Turkestan. Without manuring, without any tilling worth mentioning, they can take two, even three crops of maize, wheat and rice a year. And in the orchards grow all kinds of lovely fruits in such quantities as to make a Norwegian gasp. Nor does fruit cost much. For ten cents you can get baskets full.

Through the oasis flows the Aksu Daria which, like all the rivers of Turkestan, is cloudy grey in colour and thick with mud. Yet Aksu is supposed to mean 'clear water'.

I will not pretend that I was always longing for home and Norway while we were driving from oasis to oasis round the Takla Makan. There was no time for that. But, if I thought of Norway, it was always with a fierce longing for clear water, for water that was cold and fresh. Sometimes, as I sat up on that load of petrol tins, the wiping away of sweat and sand would grow mechanical and for a while I would be tramping through heath and bog and hearing the soft squelch of rubber boots coming away from mud, and my soaking trousers would be slapping deliciously on knee and thigh . . .

From Aksu to Kashgar the country was relatively flat; the road was mostly a built road and sometimes even paved. By this time we had moved down two storeys: that is to say, we had emptied two layers of the petrol tins in filling up the lorry's tank, for petrol stations were by no means frequent on that route.

The drivers had done well. They took fourteen days for the journey, and anyone who knows the road will agree you cannot quarrel with that. Also the distance was close on 1,700 miles. On the last day of the trip the drivers had an opportunity of showing their mettle, and more than once my heart was in my mouth or in my boots. But, once past the oases of Pachushov and Faisabad, we were all right and rolled into Kashgar safe and sound.

And was I glad to have got there! The stay in Tihua had done me good and my back had become considerably stronger, consequently the drive from Tihua to Kashgar had not been nearly as bad as that from Kuldsha, but I was fairly groggy all the same.

My yellow lady friend gave me a dazzling smile at parting and I was delivered over, complete with passport and papers, at the police-station. An officer took charge of me, and, of course, straightway put me in a cell—plus the usual attendant with rifle and fixed bayonet.

I sat on the mud bank with my head in my hands, tired and worn out, and horribly stiff in every limb. My back was hurting more than ever. I had bombarded the officer with questions about an English consulate and about my former companions. Of the latter he appeared to have no knowledge, and as for a British Consulate: '*Nie, nie* . . . *Angliski nieto!*'

To tell the truth I was rather shuddering at the thought of what lay ahead of me, more or less crippled as I was: having to spend perhaps weeks draped across a horse's back up in the Himalayas with those unpleasant soldiers for company, and then, most probably, to be left to my own devices at one place or another away up on the Indian frontier where anything might happen.

But there was one thing I had learned: as a last resort one could always try invoking the Russians and, if necessary, I would do that even in Kashgar.

In the evening I was taken out for an airing in the courtyard. From there you looked out across a confusion of flat, grey roofs, just as in all the towns in Turkestan, but at one point in that jumble I saw something fluttering against the sky, something that appeared to be red, white and blue: a flag! And it was a flag that I had seen before—Great Britain's flag. No Moslem hoists the Union Jack over his roof-top, I thought, so there must be a British Consulate in Kashgar after all, and those suspicious swine had been making a fool of me the whole time.

I pointed to the flag and tried to make my guard understand that I wanted to go there, but he was as obstinate as an old goat:

'*Nie, nie . . . Angliski nieto.*'

No Englishmen indeed! Then why in hell was the Union Jack fluttering there so invitingly?

The soldier shook his head regretfully and kept on reiterating, '*Angliski nieto.*'

Disappointment and exasperation coming on top of four and a half months' accumulated irritation at all the lies and nonsense with which these people had tried to stuff me, now made my temper boil over. All the strongest expressions I knew in Norwegian, Swedish, Russian and English, plus a number of more than doubtful Moslem words, poured from me in an incoherent stream, which ended by my shoving my head into the guard's face and roaring: '*Konsulstovo Rossiskai!*'

That worked. Thoroughly frightened, he ran off to fetch his officer, and when he came, I went through my repertoire for his benefit and even added to it. He too capitulated at once to *Konsulstovo Rossiskai* and ordered the guard to take me to—the British Consulate!

I have seldom looked and been so dirty and shabby as when I strode through the streets of Kashgar with my guard. Dust, dirt and sweat were caked all over my hair, clothes and face. But it is seldom that I have felt so joyful. At last I would meet people who would give me a straight answer, and an Englishman would presumably help in whatever way he could.

The citizens of Kashgar classified me at once as a sinister bandit, and they had no difficulty in seeing that I was also a *parang*. But what did I care if they did spit after me? I just strode along after my guard.

Soon we came to the Consulate which was surrounded by a whitewashed wall. England's coat of arms shone above the gateway, outside which sat a number of Indian soldiers in chalk-white uniforms and with tall white turbans on their heads. At the sight of us they sprang to their feet, lined up, and then, with their backsides in the air and black faces down towards the ground, they chorused:

'*Salam aleikom, Sahib!*'

'*Angliski!*' said my guard sourly, pointed through the gateway into the courtyard, turned on his heel and vanished.

With slow, almost devout steps I walked in through the gateway and looked round. On one side was a tennis court, on the other some cosy little houses; facing me was a green lawn and beyond it another gateway into the Consular building itself, and on the lawn stood two men. One of them was white, a tall strongly-built chap in flannel trousers and white shirt, his hair fair, his face coppery brown from sun and wind. He came smiling towards me:

'How do you do! Welcome to Kashgar!'

When we shook hands, I could feel his grip right down to my knees. I was so overjoyed that I felt almost delirious, and I am afraid that I behaved rather idiotically as he led me inside. A short order—and there was a white-clad servant with a tray of glasses and a decanter. The Consul mixed a dark one for me, a light one for himself, and then made me gape by saying, as he smilingly raised his glass:

'*Skål, Wille! Alt for Norge*—and England,' he added. We drank out.

With that Eric Shipton sent me straight off to have a bath.

10. Eric Shipton's Guest

SITTING IN THE drawing-room of the British Consulate in Kashgar with a misty glass of whisky-and-soda and a box of English cigarettes in front of me, I told them the tale of my tribulations. Beside Mr Shipton, the Consul-General, there was the Vice-Consul, Dr Sylway, and his wife. Sylway was Anglo-Indian and Mrs Sylway was Swedish and a missionary.

Perhaps it sounds cheap and hackneyed to say that I felt a different person—but I did. Let someone else go through all that I had since arriving in Comrade Shun's famous republic, and by the time he gets to Kashgar perhaps he will notice that the smell of Moslem is no longer so horribly obtrusive as it used to be. Perhaps he will begin to suspect that this is possibly due to the fact that he himself is beginning to spread very much the same odour around his own person. Then let that someone indulge in an orgy with hot water and soap, let him be given clean, light clothes, have a good meal served at a table with gleaming

white tablecloth, let him be put to bed in silk pyjamas and
sleep for ten hours between cool, clean sheets . . . then
I think that someone will feel as I did.

The best thing of all, perhaps, was that I was able to sit
there and talk Norwegian. What a pleasure that was being
able to talk without putting my jaws out of joint with
Russian and Moslem sounds. After I had told my tale as
well as I could, Mrs Sylway translated it for the other two.

Mr Shipton laughed at my description of the officers in
Tihua, for he knew the kind well. Once or twice he used a
pause to produce one of the few Norwegian words he knew:
'Skål!' And at the end, when I had finished, he said to me:

'All right, Willie. You'll get to Little Norway, don't worry.
But just now you must stay here for a bit and we'll see if
we can't get you back into shape.'

From him I learned how the police had come with my
companions' passports and demanded visas for India for
them. He had said that he wanted to see the lads first, but
the police would have none of it. The papers had gone to
and fro for several days until eventually the lads came to
the Consulate themselves. They had orders to leave Kashgar within a week—which they did. They had told him
all about me, and that I badly needed help—but now I
was here myself and all sorrows were forgotten.

I spent a month in Kashgar, and now I look back on those
days as some of the happiest of my life. Everybody at the
Consulate did their utmost to give me a good time, but my
main thanks go to the Consul-General himself.

Eric Shipton, of course, was no ordinary consul. His
name is known all over the world and there are few who
have not read one or other of the books he has written
about his great climbs. He has climbed in the Himalayas,

in Europe—including Norway—and he has planted his
feet on the tops of Kilimanjaro and Ruwenzori, the two
highest mountains in Africa. He has led several of the
assaults and reconnaissances on Everest. To me he was
one of the finest people I have ever met. Physically he was
magnificent, and he had all the best qualities one associates
with an English gentleman. As a host he was incomparable
and he made my stay in Kashgar unforgettable.

Dr and Mrs Sylway, both kindness itself, were the only
other Europeans at the Consulate, but there were other
very kindly people. For example, there was a Persian with
the resonant name of Raza-Ali, a tubby genial round person
weighing well over 200 pounds. I never saw him except
dressed as for a wedding in a dazzlingly white, freshly-
ironed suit of European cut, white turban, patent-leather
shoes, and carrying a walking stick with a silver handle.
His great friend, an Indian from Karachi with the no less
resonant name of K. J. Limbro-Wala was the exact opposite
of the Persian—at any rate in appearance. The only elegant thing about that small, dried-up, dark little man was
his gold-rimmed spectacles. The Persian was the cashier,
the Indian the chief clerk of the Consulate, and the two
of them gave Dr Sylway and me several good trouncings
at bridge. There were two Chinese, Chu and Wai, one the
secretary and the other the clerk. Both were from Peiping
and very decent chaps. Chu was a tall, skinny being with
a passion for chess, and if ever I had a spare moment, there
he was with his board and his men. Naturally, I got soundly
beaten every time, but it was fun all the same. Thomas
Wai was about my own age, and we became quite good
friends.

The white-clad Indian soldiers were men from a Hunza
Company of the Gilgit Scouts, and they wore the regi-

mental badge, a silver ibex head, in their turbans. Most of them were slim strong chaps and one and all friendly and polite. We got on well together.

And, heavens, I mustn't forget Lakpah Tsjinsjing Sherpa, a Tibetan and a true son of the Himalayas. He was Mr Shipton's own boy and had been with him on Mount Everest in 1933. Since then he had followed his master like a shadow. He was small, thin and short-legged but incredibly strong. He had never been to school, but nonetheless he wrote in my autograph book in five different languages each with its own alphabet: Tibetan, Nepalese, Nazal, Hindustani and tolerable English. Lakpah's devotion to Eric Shipton was quite boundless.

One day I got a fright. A day or two after my arrival, a Sinkiang soldier came marching up with the very definite announcement that in three days time I was to be accompanied to the Indian frontier by the Military Police. To this Mr Shipton sent the equally categorical reply that that was damned nonsense. The soldier was to tell his superiors that Mr Skrede's back was in too bad a state for such a journey, and that the British Consul protested and demanded permission for Mr Skrede to remain at least a month. The soldier departed, but was back again in no time and this time with a very definite order. Good back or bad, the strange Anglee was to be there when the police started for Mintaka Pass in three days' time. *Basta!*

This was a bit irritating, but Mr Shipton said very calmly that it would all arrange itself. 'We'll pay a visit to the Russians,' he said.

The following day Mr Shipton, Dr Sylway and I drove in the Consulate's fine carriage behind its even finer horses through the town to the Russian Consulate. What a place that was: swimming pool, tennis court and all imaginable luxuries. There was even a radio station and a hospital there.

The Russians gave us a friendly welcome and were very interested in my little trip. For my part I was glad to be able to say some nice things about the help I had had from their fellow-countrymen in Kuldsha. That obviously delighted them and they promised to help me—and they did.

Dr Mickovitch of the Russian hospital there gave my back a thorough examination, and to my great joy told me that in time it would be quite all right again. But he said, too, that even after a month's rest at Kashgar, it would not stand up to the trip across the Karakorum without the support of a leather corset, and he promised he would get me one.

The Russian Consul and Dr Mickovitch each wrote a declaration which were sent to the police, and Mr Shipton said with a smile that when they had read them they would keep quiet for a while.

Later we were invited to stay to lunch with the Russians. Never before or since have I ever seen such extravagant quantities of food and drink. By comparison a Swedish *smörgåsbord* would be short commons.

The following day the police sent word that I had been granted permission for a month's stay.

The British Consulate in Kashgar lay on a slope on the fringe of the town. From its veranda you looked out over a confusion of flat mud roofs. Among that jumble of ugly and ramshackle little houses and bazaar shops one or two temples stood out in solitary and incongruous beauty, while here and there a grey Sinkiang poplar would rise up out of the jumble.

The oasis round the town was large and well cultivated,

criss-crossed with water-channels fringed with tamarisk, and, like the other oases of Turkestan, fantastically fertile. Through the oasis and the town flows the Kashgar Darja, dirty and grey, sluggish and listless, a true river of Sinkiang.

From time immemorial Kashgar has been of great importance for commerce between China, India and Russia and the other countries of the West. Caravan routes fan out from it in all directions; one leads westwards over the Alai Mountains to Samarkand and Bokhara, another northwards across the Celestial Mountains to Kazakstan. Two roads run eastwards to Central China—the one by which we had come from Tihua, and another which goes round the oases along the Kwenlun. To the south, across the inhospitable ranges of the Karakorum and Himalayas also go two routes: one along the frontier with Pamir and across the Mintaka Pass to Srinagar in Kashmir, the other goes farther east by Yarkand to Leh in Ladakh.

In Kashgar the population is more mixed and the throng in the bazaar streets more colourful than perhaps anywhere else in Sinkiang. The Chinese are if anything even less in evidence than elsewhere, but to make up for it there are representatives of many other Eastern peoples who, together with the gentle Turkoman, fill the dusty dung-strewn streets. These swarm with bearded Tadjeks and Khirgiz; haughty Afghans stalk along proudly; black-haired, flat-nosed Tibetans and sinister Tungans complete the picture.

Kashgar is a city of caravans, and the camels, jogging through its streets in long strings, fitted in so well with life in Sinkiang. Sedately and slothfully they set one leg in front of the other—if I don't come today, perhaps I shall come tomorrow. They looked nice and cosy, and, of course, I had to go up to a muzzle and pat it as though it had been a good-tempered horse. That's a thing you don't do more than once, for the putrid stench of a camel's breath soon teaches you to keep at a respectful distance.

There were innumerable donkeys jogging through the streets with water-containers and loads of peat, reeds and brushwood. The drivers belaboured and kicked them and shouted appallingly.

The populace was unfriendly, almost hostile in its attitude to the English and all other foreigners with the exception of the Russians. It was a thing that had grown much worse in recent years.

But I had a grand time in Kashgar. I could go for walks in the garden with Mrs Sylway, and how wonderful it was to be there talking a Scandinavian tongue and walking under trees whose branches were laden with figs and apricots! Mrs Sylway told me about the work of the Swedish missionaries in Kashgar and Yarkand, of the hard struggle they had had against superstition, ignorance and fanaticism, and of what they had done in the way of looking after the sick. Slowly but surely, however, the authorities had driven them out, and now she was alone with strict orders to confine her work of enlightenment and teaching to the area of the Consulate. Allah now was sovereign there.

Lakpah Tsjinsjing Sherpa was omnipresent, ever obliging and always willing to tell me about Tibet and the Himalayas. He told me of his adventures in the mountains with Mr Shipton, and of his curious homeland into which no disbeliever might set foot, but where every year thousands of the faithful make pilgrimages to the holy mountains which are the abode of the divine ones. He told me about reincarnation, how even the poorest wretch, if he be pious and humble enough, may, in each existence, come nearer to Nirvana. The pilgrimages to the most sacred of all mountains, miraculous Kailas, was a step in the journey to Nirvana. The staunchest, those who managed to complete the pilgrimage round the mountain on their knees, had assured themselves of a good start in the everlasting rush for eternal happiness. The gods were just, and those who were in such a hurry that they walked the miles of road round Kailas, they too in the fullness of time would resign themselves to taking a place at the back of the queue for the abode of the gods.

But best of all Lakpah liked to talk about his master, Mr Shipton, and Lakpah was worried about the future. He knew his master, could read him like an open book, and knew perfectly well also that there was a great war going on in the world, a war in which his Sahib's country was fighting for its life. Even though Lakpah realized that a British Consul cannot just leave his post because there is a war on, he realized that beneath his Sahib's calm exterior burned a flame that would drive him to go to the fight. And Lakpah could not go with him there. His Sahib had told him that.

When that evil day came, Lakpah was going to go to Darjeeling. There he would wait, for he knew that his Sahib had lost his heart for all time to Mount Everest and, if he were to live, he would return to it. Then Lakpah would be his boy again.

Lakpah Tsjinsjing Sherpa was in many ways a hard nut. His coarse black hair, his coal-black eyes and hard bony face gave him the appearance of a godforsaken bandit, yet it was wonderful to see his undisguised emotion whenever he spoke of the possibility of being parted from his beloved Sahib. On many an occasion he wept so that the tears were coursing down his cheeks.

Nothing gave me so much pleasure as to sit and listen to Mr Shipton himself telling of his adventures in the Himalayas, of the obsession of his struggle with Everest. I was spellbound when I heard of the long and painstaking preparations, of the toil involved in moving the base for the assault bit by bit nearer the top, and of how the elements could upset all calculations in a moment: snow-storms, avalanches and the incalculable monsoon; the long enervating time of waiting, and the hectic excitement when the decisive attack could at last be launched.

'Life has many fine things to offer a man,' Shipton said, 'but few can be compared with the grand tussle with the elements the Himalayas present, where even defeat leaves you filled with happiness.'

One evening we were sitting on the veranda with a whisky and soda. Mr Shipton had sat silent for a long time, gazing dreamily into the dust-haze in the south which veiled the distant snowpeaks of the Karakorum from us. Now he's on Mount Everest again, I told myself. Then, suddenly he said:

'Norway's beautiful!' And with that he began speaking of Store Skagastølstind and a lot of other peaks in Norway which, I am ashamed to say, I scarcely knew existed.

I did not go out on my own much in Kashgar, but one day Lakpah and I went for a tour of the bazaar and there I had a wonderful encounter with one of the inhabitants. I was able to understand a little of what he said, Lakpah helped with a bit more, and the chap was a wonder with his fingers. All at once he pointed at a bevy of girls nearby, and made use of certain gestures with such virtuosity it was impossible not to understand his meaning.

'*Salam, chai safed aka*! (Peace, dear good white brother.)' he began. And so gradually we were told the following tale of woe.

Oh, he was so poor, so miserably poor . . . yes, the sorriest marmot up in Sarikol was better off than he. Besides, he was in the ignominious position of not having a *chanum* in his *chana*, no woman in his house. In that part of the world it cost a fortune to get yourself a wife. His special dearly beloved was no cheap one either, but now by inhuman industry he had scraped together so much that he only lacked one dollar to fix the deal—Oh, *Allah il Allah*! Did the foreign Sahib not think it a shame and a misery that he must renounce the rapturous felicity of love merely because he lacked one lousy dollar?

I was by no means flush, but all the same I fished out a Sinkiang dollar and gave it to the man who was profuse in his thanks: '*Bahnjama, behujama, frengi aka sjeriff*! (Thank you, thank you, good foreign friend!)'

But now the fellow had tasted blood. He chattered away and gestured even more vehemently than before. In the stream of words there was one that kept cropping up: '*Tsjal-jab, tsjal-jab.*' I had no idea what a *tsjal-jab* was, and Lakpah just stood there smiling ironically. It was obvious, however, that the man was suggesting a business deal of some kind: if he got just one more dollar he would fix a tsjal-jab for the Sahib.

Having managed to get a dollar it seemed to me that he ought to have been content, and in the end we got rid of him.

Thomas Wai laughed when I told him about it, and he explained what a *tsjal-jab* was. We call it a tart.

According to what Wai told me, morals were fairly free in those parts. There was, for example, a girl of under fifteen at the Consulate and she had already been married five times without being widowed. There was one man who over the years had had more than a hundred wives. Nevertheless, he said, morals in Kashgar must be considered relatively high for Sinkiang. In the oases along the Kwen-lun there was really no morality at all as such. There you changed wives just as it suited you, and by the time she was fifteen every girl had had dozens of lovers.

Perhaps there was a bridal night in that poor Moslem's *chana*. But perhaps he just had a good laugh over the credulous Anglee. How do I know?

11. Ready for the Himalayas

I CAME TO Kashgar on September 2nd. Although Mr Shipton thought that a month was the least I needed to get into reasonable shape for the strenuous trip across the mountains, he also told me straight away that somewhere around October 1st was as late as one dare wait. Winter would be approaching then, and snowstorms might come at any time and make the whole thing impossible.

He had a plan to send me with a trader's caravan going into India, and there were endless parleyings with the Commissar about that. On this point, however, the Commissar would not yield. The military police and none other were to make sure that the suspicious Anglee went over the frontier into India.

Mr Shipton sent a telegram to Gilgit, the nearest British military establishment on the Indian side, asking for a man to be sent up to the frontier to meet me. Sending a telegram from Kashgar to Gilgit is not a very simple matter: first a courier must be sent on horseback to Mishgar, which is the terminus of the telegraph in India, and to get to Mishgar

132

the courier has a good fourteen days travelling across the mountains. Among other things, he must cross both the Chichiklik Pass and the Mintaka Pass, both of which are over 16,000 feet.

Mr Shipton sketched the whole route for me: first fourteen days riding to Mishgar; then another good week in the Karakorums, through the mountainous Hunza country to Gilgit, and from there ten to twelve days more across the western Himalayas to Srinagar in Kashmir, from where there was a motor road to the nearest railway station at Rawalpindi.

'The whole road is through wild mountainous country,' he said, 'and even you who come from Norway and are used to mountains will find things there a little different. To manage this trip you must be able to ride. Can you?'

The only time I had ever tried was in my early childhood, when I had clambered up on to the back of an aged farm horse which was so steady that an old woman could have ridden it blindfold. I had to admit despondently that unfortunately I could not ride.

'Okay,' said Mr Shipton, 'we'll teach you!'

He drew up a programme for my days: riding, and a little cautious tennis, together with other training, to get me back into shape. And, as he smilingly put it: 'I shall ask Mr Wai if he will try to teach you to maltreat my mother tongue a little less.' Thomas Wai did his best, though I am afraid I was an unsatisfactory pupil, for there were far too many things claiming my attention.

One day I went up to the Russian hospital to be fitted for my leather corset, and that was a pantomime. I had to hang stark naked holding by my hands to a pole fixed on the wall and with my toes just touching the floor, while Dr Mickovitch tied me up with gauze and plaster of Paris

to get a mould for the shape of the corset. While in this
position, a Moslem walked in for some reason or other.
I don't know what he thought when he saw a naked white
man hanging on the wall, but perhaps he had been told
that Europeans went in for crucifixion and horrors of that
kind, for he went as pale as a corpse. He stood there swaying, his mouth wide open, and I could see his pink uvula
going to and fro like the air valve on a gas generator, then
with a screech of '*Allah il Allah*' he fainted flat on the floor.
Dr Mickovitch laughed and told me that many of the
Moslems are squeamish and can't stand much.

That corset was a grand affair and a great help when I
began learning to ride. The beginnings were very cautious
with a Hunza leading the horse round and round the
sports ground. It did not take long, however, before I
could manage on my own and soon I even plucked up
courage to try a very short gallop. Having reached that
stage I always accompanied Mr Shipton on his early
morning rides.

What grand fun they were, and what a wonderful feeling it was to know that you had full control of your body
and could follow the horse in all its movements.

First we would ride through the swarming crowds in the
streets of Kashgar, then a brisk gallop across the plain,
through tall reed beds and water-channels and streams
with the water spurting up around us, down avenues of
trees scattering camels and donkeys in all directions, and
finally back home to porridge, toast and pitch black coffee.

Some people will tell you that it isn't a sport to let
yourself be transported about on the back of a horse, but
there I can't agree. And there's nothing like a ride before
breakfast to give you an appetite.

Both Lakpah and Wai used to boast of the quantities of

game there were in the hills west of Kashgar and one day the entire Consulate set off on a hare shoot. There was Mr Shipton, Dr Sylway, Raza Ali, Limbro-Wala, Chu, Wai, Lakpah and myself, all of us equipped with gum-boots and shotguns. We set out early in the morning in a Ford lorry.

West of the town we saw several hundred men building a new road. As far as I understand it, it was the Russians who paid the piper. In a little while we reached a valley down which the river Kizil wound and twisted. This valley of the Kizil was fantastically beautiful with its sheer mountains on either side, luxuriant greenery on the valley floor and bright glowing colours on the mountainsides. The road continued as a caravan road up the valley and across the Alai Mountains to Samarkand. That must have been the way that Marco Polo had once come with his camels and donkeys. And Djengis Khan and Timur Lenk had probably also marked it out with heads set up on stakes.

We were to shoot at a place where the river divided leaving a large flat island in the middle of its two arms. It was on this island that all the hares were supposed to be and to reach it we had to put on our rubber boots and wade across the Kizil which was pretty fast-flowing. Raza Ali, of course, was in his inevitable white suit and he was a little reluctant to venture out into the dirty-grey muddy water. Lakpah, the ever-obliging, offered to carry him across, and a fine sight the slight figure of the Sherpa made wading up to his waist in the water with the huge Persian on his back. Raza brandished a gun in one hand, his walking-stick in the other; then suddenly Lakpah stumbled and, to everybody's delight, the two went splash into the muddy water. Raza Ali was a bit put out, but Lakpah just beamed as he always did.

There were plenty of hares, and in quite a short time we had shot a score of them.

On other occasions Dr Sylway, Lakpah and I tried our hand at duck shooting. There were extensive ricefields round the town which were flooded, and a lot of ground was overgrown with reeds. These reeds were the haunt of duck. Lakpah used to ferret about in them, while Sylway and I banged away at the birds which flew up.

The Hunza boys had acquired the Englishman's taste for football, but unfortunately my back only allowed me to play a spectator's part. Polo had also been popular, but the way they played it proved to be a little too lively: two of the scouts had lost their lives in a match and so the Consul had forbidden the game. All the same I did see it played, though with donkeys instead of ponies. And what a game that was! The donkeys flew in all directions except that in which their riders wanted them to go.

Like most of their race the Indian servants were appallingly idle. Each boy had just his own special little job: one cleaned shoes, another helped the cook, and so on, and they were most reluctant to turn their hands to anything else. One evening I noticed that the Consulate's flag was still hoisted after sundown and so I went up and took it down. The next evening the flag was again up after sunset, and when the boy was asked why he had shirked his job, he replied that Sahib Skrede had done it the previous evening and so he had thought there was no need for him to bother.

Among Mr Shipton's books I found Peter Fleming's *News from Tartary* in which he tells of the trip he and a Swiss woman journalist made from Peiping through Turkestan to Kashgar and on across the Karakorums to Srinagar. I used to take a drink out on to the veranda and spell my way through the vivid descriptions there, which gave me an idea of what awaited me, for my way was to be the same as theirs.

That veranda had not always been a peaceful place. It was there that the Consulate's doctor was killed during the riots in 1934, and the wife of the former Consul-General, Thomson-Glover, got a bullet in her arm.

Finally the day came when I had to say goodbye to my friends in Kashgar.

I had taken Wai's advice and sent most of my stuff ahead of me with a caravan for Mishgar. This included my diaries, autograph book and a camera which Wai had got me. If I hadn't done that I evidently ran a good chance of things 'going astray' during the final passport control and customs examination at Tasj Kurghan.

Mr Shipton gave me final advice and instructions drawing a map of the critical part of the road up at the frontier for me. Just in case there was no one there from Gilgit to meet me I was provided with some reserve provisions, including a tin of bacon.

'If you have any trouble with your guards, just produce your bacon,' said Mr Shipton and gave a wily laugh.

On October 2nd, I went as arranged to the police-station and reported myself ready for the last stage out of Comrade Shun's territory.

12. Dead Horse Road

/\\

ONCE MORE I was in the keeping of Sinkiang soldiery.
The three specimens who comprised my escort on the first
stage of the road to Gilgit did not look very gifted, but at
least seemed comparitively good-natured. Their eyes were
set at a steep enough slant, but even so they were not
typically Chinese as had been the others with whom I had
dealt. I imagine that they were Khirgiz or something of
that kind. At any rate they were thoroughly at home in
mountains, stocky powerful chaps who stank of Sinkiang
all right! They understood not one word of what I said,
and sign language was our only means of conversing—at
least at the beginning.

There can be few places where the distinction between
horse and horse is so crass as in Turkestan. You see well-
groomed bloodhorses so lovely that you quiver with joy at
the sight of them, and caravan ponies so shabby and
emaciated, as to make the most indifferent flinch. There
lies a social gulf between the proud Badakshan stallion and

the ever famished, everlastingly toiling proletarians of the mountain roads.

The policemen's horses looked pretty poor creatures, and the one I was to ride no better. However, as it and I were to be buddies for a couple of weeks, I went up to introduce myself and disentangled a bit of its dirty fore-lock. Sulky and disobliging, it jerked its head away: obviously these horses did not get much in the way of pats or petting.

'Sociable you are certainly not,' said I, 'but you had better have a name even so. I shall call you Mohammed.'

There was also a small girl going with us. She sat on her horse quite enveloped in a rose-coloured quilted kaftan, which allowed only the tip of a turned-up nose to be seen. Thus there were five horses in our caravan as we emerged from Kashgar and set out sedately across the plain.

That first day we got no farther than the little cluster of houses at Yapsjan, for one of the horses took ill, and there we spent the night in what the Turkomans call a *liangar*: on a hillside was a rectangular little field, at the top of the slope a covered ledge on which we slept, below it a half-shelter for the animals.

Throughout the whole of the following day we rode through a uniform countryside where you saw nothing but interminable sand dunes and the dirty-grey bed of a stream with a tamarisk bush here and there. We spent the night in the oasis of Yangi Hissar, and then, on the evening of the third day, we reached the little oasis of Igiz Yar. Here a number of Turkis joined us. The police-men got hold of several more horses and on these loaded oats and other provisions for the animals. It was thus quite a good-sized caravan of some twenty beasts which left Igiz Yar. From there we could see mountains ahead of us, and it was not long before we were out of the sand dunes and had come into a glen. At the foot of the mountains lay some of the usual mud huts and a few poplar and apricot trees.

The glen was roomy enough at the start: there were green slopes, a few woods here and there, and the stream wound along lazy and sluggish. But the glen soon narrowed, and it was not long before the stream had whipped itself into a raging little torrent.

Slowly the Gilgit road unfolded. I sat my horse and kept finding it hard to believe my eyes—I don't know what I wouldn't have given to have had a camera. Soon the road took to a narrow shelf in the mountainside 200 feet or so above the foaming torrent, with the rock dropping sheer beneath it and rising almost equally sheer for over a thousand feet on the other side. Then it descended down a narrow ravine to the valley floor and some rapids. Somehow or other we managed to get across, and then we had to clamber up an even narrower ravine on the other side and up along another narrow shelf. Of course there were many places where you could not ride but had to lead your horse behind you.

The first time we crossed the river I thought that my travels were going to end there in that devilish hole, that in a moment or two the entire caravan would be sent swirling and shrieking down the rapids. But the policemen just went slap in so that the spray spurted up round them. Their wild shouts were nothing to go by—that was just something that went with the scene, though perhaps at that moment they were more savage than usual. I realized that there was nothing much I could do about it except to trust to Mohammed. And Mohammed followed the horse in front of him without an instant's hesitation. I had to pull my feet out of the stirrups for the greyish-yellow water was foaming close under the brute's belly. I could feel that Mohammed was fighting against the pressure of the current for all he was worth, and actually stamping his hooves down to get a hold on the uneven bottom. We got across all right.

So it continued throughout the day. I believe we crossed that torrent every five hundred yards, and I learned to admire the small shaggy Turkoman horses for their ability to make their way whether fording a rushing river or climbing a stiff ravine. They must be the most sure-footed creatures in the world. I know that here and there in the ravines and gullies lay the skeletons of horses to show that many of those maltreated and abused drudges had succumbed while plying the Gilgit road; but all went well for us and I have many a grateful thought to Dr Mickovitch for getting me that leather corset and to Mr Shipton for having me taught to ride.

Gradually the ground began to rise more steeply and by evening we were fairly high up the mountain. We spent the night in the open. I was stiff in every limb and as tired as could be, but nevertheless I tackled the pepper and mutton with voracious appetite. The view was magnificent, but it could not hold me for long—I was too tired for that.

The following day we continued. At first across an upland plateau, then down into another valley, where we again had to negotiate a ford which, if possible, was even worse than any we had had before.

Having laboured through a narrow bluffy glen we emerged on to another plateau. There we met a camel caravan, and I wondered what would have happened if we had encountered it in the narrowest part of the glen.

There were various kinds of birds up there, and we saw

herds of odd-looking goats and sheep; some had horns like giant corkscrews. Besides these, there were innumerable marmots which sat in the mouths of their holes and hissed at us.

Then we began to encounter the Gilgit road's own special sign-posts: the half-eaten bodies of horses. Greyish-white vultures swung round us on heavy wings.

At one point my policemen sought variety in a little hunting. We had put up some white birds about the size of a capercailzie and the guns came into action. They were not very good shots and brought nothing down, but all the same it developed into a lively hunt which showed what good horsemen they were and demonstrated the incredible skill of those horses on rough ground.

We came to a place called Aktala where there was a cluster of round felt tents, yurts or *kibitkas*, as the Khirgiz call them. Thick felt rugs are laid over a framework of thin wooden stakes—about the thickness of a fishing rod—and tied with cords round the outside. These yurts looked quite substantial and were indeed fairly roomy. The floors inside consist of several layers of rugs laid over a thick layer of moss, and the fact that there were plenty of lice in those rugs was a thing I could do nothing about unfortunately.

It was devilish cold in Aktala, but the mountain air was pure and fresh, and how lovely it was to be free of the myriad flies of Turkestan.

Down in the valleys I had seen quite a number of woods, mostly fir, but now we were above the tree-line and there was nothing but bare expanses and screes and huge rocks to be seen. To the west we could see the first of the 22,000-to 23,000-foot giants which flank the Gilgit road—snow-capped Mustagh Ata, father of the mountains and sovereign of the Sarikol.

It was in these wilds that we met yaks for the first time. Yaks can only live in the high mountains, above ten thousand feet. They have heavy bodies, short legs and long, straggly hair which sweeps down to their heels and makes them look like hay-cocks perched among the stones. Their appearance was terrifying, and for all their great size they hopped about the mountainsides as easily and lightly as any goat.

Then we came to Kashka Su, and there too were some yurts. Otherwise there was just the bare savage mountain: rugged and as cold as charity. There was no getting away from the fact that it was a draughty and dreary spot, but all the same I felt more at home than among the flies and dust in the intolerable heat of the plain. We were allowed into one of the yurts, got a fire going with dried yak-dung and were relatively comfortable.

Shortly after leaving Kashka Su the road became ghastly: long, steep slopes that pumped the guts out of you, and no sooner had we surmounted that and got up on to a plateau than we had to slither down precipitous bluffs on the other side. After that we plunged straight into another glen as wild and narrow as any we had traversed, and through it ran yet another swift and fierce torrent. Again we began those nerve-racking fordings every few hundred yards, then the road began to climb once more. What faced us now was one of the worst bits of the entire trip: the ascent to the Chichiklik Pass.

The road wound its way upwards in an infinity of bends, then into a gigantic scree of boulders as large as houses. Here the skeletons of horses lay at frequent intervals, and an occasional small cairn, some with a horse's tail as a decoration, proclaimed that there lay the mortal remains of a man.

Our wretched horses had a ghastly time of it. Even though we dismounted and walked, they still had the baggage to carry, and it was obvious that the great height and the thinness of the air affected them worse than us. It was pitiable to watch them toiling up step by step, then suddenly halting with all four legs straddled and their flanks heaving in the effort to get air.

Pity for a horse, however, is an unknown sentiment on the Chichiklik Pass. I thought I would retch when the Turkis began jabbing them on the muzzle with sharp iron spikes so that the blood ran. I have been told that this is not cruelty to animals, but a humane blood-letting which helps the poor brutes to support the rarity of the atmosphere! Perhaps it is, but it looks too horrible for words.

For hundreds and hundreds of years caravans have been passing between Kashmir and Kashgar. To many people that is a nice romantic thought, but not to those who have crossed the Chichiklik Pass and had a glimpse of the hell which that trading route has been for thousands of tormented ponies who just had to toil and endure it all and had no Allah to call upon.

The pale skeletons tell a grim story, but they are not the only road signs in the Chichiklik. Along the whole pass there are dark-brown splodges on the stones. Once they were fresh streaming blood. Each drop is a message from the trembling horses that have foundered there.

Chichiklik lies somewhat over fifteen thousand feet above sea level and is the second highest pass on the Gilgit Road. There is only the Mintaka Pass which is higher and worse. The descent from that pass was bad enough, but it was not so ghastly as the climb up.

Once again we emerged into a large upland plateau, and there we came to a large Khirgiz camp, an *aul* as it is called. These roving people of the mountains had settled down there for a while and put up a whole little town of yurts. There were large herds of yaks grazing in the vicinity. In between the yurts were great piles of dried yak droppings which is the only fuel the Khirgiz have. Some of the yurts were decked out with coloured ribbands over the pieces of carpeting: social distinctions exist pretty well everywhere.

The Kara Khirgiz are small of stature, but they look strong and spirited. The men go in for thick felt boots and quilted tunics reaching half way down their legs and they usually have a bit of rope tied round their waists. Most are as bearded as shoe-brushes, and their black round hats help to make them look fierce. The women wear flowered jackets and have huge white cloth-pokes on their heads. When they squat outside their yurts meditating, their queer headgear appears larger than all the rest of the woman. I didn't think they were much to look at.

The yak-cows, which were obviously a very mixed lot, were the most peculiar-looking animals. It looked as though it had originally been the intention to create a goat, but that the result had grown several times larger than had been intended and also had not turned out quite right in other ways. That being so, there was nothing for it but to rehash it and try to make a serviceable cow out of it. That, too, hadn't come off. In sheer desperation a horse's tail was planted on the brute, and to this day the yak is a weird mixture of all three.

The Khirgiz gave us a friendly welcome. We were even invited to spend the night in the chieftain's own *kibitka,* and naturally we—that is to say the policemen and I—said thank you very much. As a result we lost touch with the others.

There was nothing wrong with those mountain people's sense of hospitality, nor did I see any sign of the hostility which was always in the air when I was in the company of Turkis. All the chaps in that *aul* were merry rascals who laughed and guffawed and made no end of a noise. It was a pity that I didn't understand a word of what they said.

The space round the yurts was alive with frolicsome children. They were like little rabbits—all wrapped in felt and quilts, and unbelievably filthy. Some of the girls had very queer headgear with a lot of tinkling dangling trinkets. There were babies, babies everywhere, and in spite of the filth many of them were enchanting though I can't say as much of some of the young girls who sat outside one of the yurts picking lice off each other. When their luck was in and they caught one, a happy light would come into their coal-black eyes, and with beaming faces they would pop the louse into their mouths.

That evening we witnessed a demonstration of a sort of Khirgiz version of polo. Some rode horses, others yak-bulls, others again yak-cows. They were all armed with sticks and there was a cloth ball: it was a mad circus. I did not understand the rules, but the spectators were in ecstasies and they couldn't have been more worked up if they had been an English crowd watching a cup final. The surprising thing was that no arms or legs were broken.

After the match we were entertained in the chieftain's *kibitka*. This was larger than the others and was lined inside with colourful rugs. The roof was lit by a small oil lamp, there was a sort of metal basin with yak-dung burning in it which filled the tent with acrid smoke, and a large copper samovar glowed in the dim light. As well as the chieftain there were several other men, presumably sons, and a woman to every man.

My nose had accustomed itself to most things during the last few months, but never had it encountered the Sinkiang stench in so rank and concentrated a form as on that memorable evening in the chieftain's *kibitka* in Sussikleika.

It was a great evening.

After seating ourselves cross-legged in a circle on the floor, the actual meal began. The woman brought the dishes and squatted down quietly and respectfully outside the circle while we ate. The menu consisted of white tea, mutton, fat and yak-milk. The tea and milk were served in bowls which were handed round from one to the other. Yak-milk is rich and rank, but it goes down all right once you have grown accustomed to it. We picked out pieces of boiled mutton in our fingers, dipped them in fat and savoured them.

I noticed that the chieftain had a hookah prepared. A hookah is like a tall pot-bellied flower-vase with a tube coming out from the middle of it, and I knew that it was part of the etiquette for it to be passed round from man to man after a meal. Now, the Turkis in general are not so cleanly that you would notice it, but those who take Mohammed seriously will at least have the tips of their fingers and the very centre of their faces in contact with water at certain times—otherwise the Prophet is sorrowful. The Kara Khirgiz are Mohammedans officially, but in practice they are incorrigible heathens who care not a jot for the Prophet's rules. From birth till death they are most careful to avoid all forms of ablution.

No one will reproach me for not being very keen about

the idea of that hookah. To try and forestall the chieftain I attempted a diversion by fishing out of my rucksack some of the cigarettes Mr Shipton had given me, and handing them round. The policemen were well accustomed to *papyrossos* and smoked away with great gusto, but the chieftain and his men had swallowed theirs before they could get much smoke out of them.

It occurred to me that I ought perhaps to do some of my parlour tricks in return for all their hospitality, so I tried the innocent little dodge of putting a cigarette to my ear and blowing smoke out through my nose. The Khirgiz laughed loudly. Then, encouraged by my success, I transferred the cigarette to another place which you can imagine, simulated a mighty inhalation and then slowly, slowly let the smoke trickle out through my nose. That called for an absolute storm of applause. The chieftain pounded me on the back and I took the flood of words which poured from his bristly beard to mean that he thought me a hell of a chap.

It's nice to think that I was popular in one home in Sinkiang.

By the flickering light of the little oil lamp we got ourselves ready for the night, that is, we curled up as we were side by side in a circle on the rugs spread on the floor. The policemen and my hosts with their womenfolk joined the chorus of snores one by one, till only Sahib Skrede was left awake?

Many lice?

Oh, yes. I'm afraid there were, quite a lot. But neither they nor the stench managed to keep sleep away for so very long.

Nothing very noteworthy happened after leaving that

Khirgiz camp. Occasionally we met a small camel caravan, and at one point we rode for quite a long time along a huge glacier. The weather was sour and cold.

We had to negotiate a number of precipitous descents on the way into the Sarikol valley. There the road ran right close to the frontier with Pamir, and on the eleventh day after leaving Kashgar we had the little mountain town of Tasj Kurghan in sight.

13. The Pass

∧∧∧∧∧∧∧∧∧∧∧∧∧∧∧∧∧∧∧∧∧∧∧∧∧∧∧∧∧

'TASJ' MEANS pile of stones, 'kurghan', fortress. The two words together make an excellent name for that god-forsaken hole where General Shun had his last official outpost before Mintaka. 'Tasj' can also mean something else: all along the mountain roads in that part of the world cairns have been set up at fixed intervals, and the distance between two such cairns is a 'tasj', the only measure of distance known there.

The name Tasj Kurghan is a common one in Central Asia. On the map you will find towns of that name in Afghanistan, Bukhara and elsewhere, but that wretched little town in the Sarikol valley would never have figured on any map in the world had it not been made important by its customs station and passport control post.

Outside the town were some small green patches on the floor of the valley, otherwise there was nothing but screes, boulders and naked rock on all sides. Within the town walls there were both yurts and mud huts with flat roofs.

150

There were bazaar sheds and serais as well, and on the public buildings, as well as the usual clutter of Chinese characters, there was also Comrade Shun's blood red symbol.

It was there that my papers and things were to be inspected for the last time on Sinkiang territory, so it was not without a certain amount of trepidation and expectation of trouble with the authorities that I made my entry into Tasj Kurghan. There, too, I was promptly shoved in a cell and the door bolted.

There was a bunk all right, and I was tired enough to be glad to stretch out flat without more ado. In Sinkiang, however, it is never what you expect that happens. When a whole gang of officers came in and I thought to myself: 'Now there's going to be a rumpus,' there was nothing of the kind. The officers were as pleasant as they could have been. They had just come to pay me a visit. One of the policemen came along with tea and food, and afterwards we sat and smoked and had a thoroughly cosy time of it.

I chatted in a sort of English with a couple of them, though I won't go so far as to say that any of us was much the wiser for it. When they took their departure we vied with each other in cordial wishes for success for ourselves and our respective near and distant relatives. I included in my rigmarole a few words of Norwegian to the effect that I was heartily sick of their damned republic and very much looking forward to getting into India and meeting decent people again.

They never even looked at my rucksack so I could have taken Thomas Wai's camera after all. Or so I thought.

It is a good two day's ride from Tasj Kurghan to the Indian frontier up in Mintaka Pass. The Pass—also called the Pass of a Thousand Ibex—is over 16,000 feet high and notorious as the worst on the Gilgit Road. It lies right in the middle of the fantastic witches' cauldron of screes, rock and glaciers thrown up where the mighty ranges of the Karakorum, Hindukush, Kwen-lun and Tien Shan bump into each other. Not far from Mintaka is the place where China, India and Soviet Asia share a common frontier cairn. And Afghanistan is not far away either. Bam-Dunjah, the Roof of the World, is the Khirgiz' name for this merciless tract.

It was thus no wonder that I was anxious to see what things would be like in Mintaka Pass. Would there be anyone from Gilgit there to meet me? Or would I be left alone up there on the Roof of the World?

I was given a different horse to take me on from Tasj Kurghan and four new military policemen to guard me. The horse was a good little beast, but my guards were thoroughly disagreeable. Perhaps they had been a long time in Tasj Kurghan. I can well imagine that a protracted stay in that stony wilderness could put anyone into a permanently bad mood. One especially was sinister and he had a long nose and scowling eyes.

For the whole of the first day we rode through a uniform mountain landscape. In the evening we reached the little village of Dafdar, where we spent the night in a stone hut.

The second day was long and strenuous. First we crossed a plateau, then we toiled laboriously over a pass. The evening brought us to Pike, which lay in a valley with a swift mountain torrent foaming between great stones. A few miserable yurts lay hidden among huge boulders. In one of those we were to sleep, as far as I was concerned, for the last time on Chinese soil. My guards were as unsociable as ever, but we all crept into the yurt together, and the horses were tethered outside as usual.

In the early twilight I was woken up by an almighty hubbub. Before I had my eyes properly open, my guards had leaped out shouting and yelling. At once there broke out an appalling hullabaloo with shots being fired, men shouting and horses neighing. Scared and only half awake I crawled out after them, and in the semi-darkness I saw some shaggy wolves disappearing among the boulders. The guards were shooting for all they were worth.

In the confusion one of the guards had rushed out without his rifle and, without knowing how it happened, I found myself standing outside clutching this and cursing because the last bit of wolf had just disappeared and I was unable to get a shot in.

I should never have snatched up that man's rifle, however! There was a savage howl and the men were on me. I was back inside the yurt quicker than I actually appreciated.

For safety's sake the guards fired off a further series of shots and ended up with some blood-curdling howls. When they came to me their blood was up all right! They were absolutely furious, snarling and behaving like wild animals. I expected them at any moment to fly at me.

The situation was not pleasant, and feverishly I racked my brains for a possible counter measure. Heavens—I had not intended anything wrong! And who wouldn't seize hold of a gun lying ready to hand when he sees a wolf for the first time in his life? But to explain that to those half-savage oafs was easier said than done. Allah alone knows what they were imagining, but they behaved as though I had attempted to murder them all.

Suddenly I remembered Eric Shipton's advice: 'If you

have any trouble with the guards', he had said, 'produce the bacon.' Worth trying. Perhaps bacon was their favourite food.

I opened my rucksack as quickly as I could, got hold of the tin of bacon, opened it and picking up a couple of rashers held them out invitingly.

'*Baksla, tovaritch! Foksji tjaztival*'

The effect was more than fantastic, for those men couldn't have moved faster if it had been old Nick himself who had popped up out of that tin. There was a multiple scream of terror and they rushed out, so that all I saw was a confusion of arms and legs in the opening in the felt. And this time they all forgot their rifles.

When I followed them out they behaved as though they really had gone off their heads: leaping about among the boulders, tearing at their hair and calling plaintively to Allah. I tried to calm them and explain that I had intended no harm: '*Salaam—Salaam aka!*' But when I approached one, he just leaped away and howled louder than ever.

It appeared that the guards really had got two of the wolves, but one of the horses was also lying there with a torn throat and bleeding groin.

Heavens, what a fuss! It took me two hours to get our departure organized, and when at last we did get away it was a very peculiar little procession. First two of the guards, then myself in splendid isolation thirty yards or so behind, and at about the same distance behind me the other two as rear-guard.

Of course I realized at once that the idiotic commotion caused by the bacon was connected with religious superstition and, when later I told the story to the officers in Gilgit, I learned that I had touched the Moslem on his most sensitive spot, for should a Moslem come in contact with bacon (or pork) both he and any off-spring he may have will be eternally unclean and lose for all time their chance of getting into Allah's paradise.

One of the most dreadful expressions in Moslem terminology is to the effect that 'I'll stuff you inside the skin of a pig!' That, apparently, is an appalling threat and is used only between sworn enemies. He who gets that flung at him, knows that after that he must look out in case he gets a knife stuck into his guts.

We were now short of a horse, and the two poor wretches of the rear-guard had to take it in turn to walk. Fortunately it was only a couple of hours march to Mintaka Fort.

The little fort lay at the bottom of a valley, just before the ascent up to Mintaka Pass began. It contained a tiny office building and a few yurts. Even here the office was decked with red stars and frames. A solitary, surly officer with a few men—if possible even more surly—comprised the garrison.

The officer examined all my possessions with the utmost thoroughness, and I realized that Wai had been right after all. The paper on which Eric Shipton had sketched the route across Mintaka was taken despite my energetic protests. It was then, while the contents of my rucksack were strewn about the place, that I discovered to my horror that all the commotion in Pike had resulted in what for me was a grievous loss. I had left all my provisions there. My clothes and other things were in my rucksack, as well as the tobacco and cigarettes Mr Shipton had given me, but all that remained of my reserve provisions was a tiny packet of biscuits. The rest lay on the floor of the yurt in Pike.

It was doubtful whether there would be anyone to meet me up on Mintaka Pass, and in desperation I sought to explain my situation to the officer and get him to find me some provisions to take with me. But the supercilious devil just sneered. He showed considerable interest in my cigarettes, and I tried to bring off a bit of barter, but did not succeed even there.

Arrogant and supercilious, he handed me my passport.

'*Hosh-hosh!*' said he.

'To hell with you,' said I.

And with that one wretched packet of biscuits for my only supplies I left Mintaka Fort.

Strangely enough my terrified guards did not seem to have told their colleagues about me and the bacon—that I had touched bacon and was unclean, and so any who touched me would also become unclean. Perhaps they liked the idea of that fate happening to the repulsive little officer. Anyway, the two new men who comprised my escort as we rode out from Mintaka Fort were blissfully ignorant of how dangerous a person the mysterious Anglee was. They were, however, very conscious of their duty and determined that they were going to see that the suspect *parang* did leave the territories of General Shun.

The road had been rising ever since we left Tasj Kurghan and, almost as soon as we had left the fort, it became devilishly steep. We rounded a severe curve; Mintaka Fort was out of sight, and I had seen Shun do Bahn's red star for the last time.

It was a real struggle up those fierce slopes to the pass. The ascent grew steeper and steeper, breathing more and more troublesome, and the number of horses' skeletons lying grey-white and grinning along the road increased.

The new guards also knew the trick with the iron spikes.

Our poor brutes grunted and trembled as we painfully toiled up and across the Pass of a Thousand Ibex—the highest on the road and the culminating point in my mounting excitement and toil.

My thoughts were rather gloomy ones as we laboured up the last few turns. It was most probable that no one had come to meet me. It was dreadfully cold and I was in no condition for a long and arduous march in the mountains. The first symptoms of mountain sickness had appeared: breathing was difficult, my heart was going irregularly, there was a singing in my ears. To add to it all I was chafing over the loss of my provisions.

Down the slopes a merry little mountain stream came leaping. I had seen more than enough of the dirty, muddy, soup-like water of the rivers of Sinkiang, and it was encouraging and promising to see this wanton beck throwing itself from shelf to shelf and calling: 'Cheer up, Willie! Before evening you'll be in India and finished with Shun do Bahn's stinking oafs.'

At one of the last bends we suddenly bumped into two mounted Hunzas. The one in front had a Union Jack fastened to his saddle, so they were couriers with the post from Gilgit to Kashgar. Naturally, I wanted to have a chat with them, but the attempt brought my guards to life. Their bayonets were out in a flash: no question of the dangerous Anglee being allowed to talk with strangers. That ruined my only chance of learning whether or not there was anyone on the way to meet me. I could only call a greeting to Kashgar after them.

The glen widened out a little, the rise became slightly less steep, and there we had the pass: a gigantic pile of black boulders. Behind this row upon serrated row of pointed, snow-capped peaks sawed at the blue sky. Both the horse and I breathed a sigh of relief when we were up.

I saw no sign of the actual frontier being marked, but there was a tiny stone hut up there, and by this the two guards halted. One slung my rucksack down at my feet and pointed towards the mountain peaks:

'Indo!'

They did not utter a further word though both were smiling mockingly. Then one tied the bridle of my poor nag to the tail of his own, turned and both rode off back down the path. I sat down and watched them go. Not once did they look back. My horse went with its head hanging. A bend and they had vanished.

I was alone on the roof of the world.

Mountain sickness is an affliction that comes to many at about ten thousand feet. It brings with it headache and giddiness; your limbs grow heavy and you have trouble with your breathing and heart. Before Mintaka I had not noticed anything particular, except that I became very quickly tired. But there are other symptoms of mountain sickness: it makes some people dream and talk in their sleep; others see strange visions in broad daylight. I must have had a touch of it and that was why I did not properly know myself on Mintaka.

It was then three o'clock in the afternoon. The morning had been strenuous; the climb up had been a considerable strain and I soon realized that in the Pass of a Thousand Ibex the body's physical powers could not be measured by normal standards. My back was pretty painful. The leather corset was a great help on horseback, but it was too stiff to walk in, and so it had to come off.

I was determined, however, that one way or another I would get myself to Mishgar and off I set indefatigably.

From that little hut there was rough scree all the way up to the ridge that blocked the view. At the top of that ridge, however, my eyes encountered a sight that made me gasp: ahead of me lay a fantastic witches' cauldron of black boulders. Mintaka glacier lay like a gigantic plough at the end of the screes, and the gorges at either side were deep and dark. At an interminable distance were white, sky-high mountain peaks with pitch-black gullies between.

The whole picture was like a mighty wood-cut. It could have been cut in a fit of frenzy, but the hand that made it must have been both steady and brutal. Where the snow was able to lie the mountains were dazzlingly white, but the precipitous slopes were polished black. Only here and there did the black of the gorges turn into strips of dark blue—a hint of green shimmered in the glacier.

I sat down and lit a cigarette. Suddenly I was no longer a young fellow on an adventurous journey into strange lands, but a wretched little insect, the only thing alive in a soundless, timeless, endless and deathly desolate world.

Karakorum means 'Black Mountains'. The name can stand. But could they not just as well have been called the mountains of death or stillness?

There was not even the peep of a bird to be heard, not so much as a faint swish from a distant stream, not a fly buzzed to show that something else was alive. Not a miserable blade of grass or a patch of moss on a stone had found life possible in Mintaka Pass. Even the sky, in which there wasn't so much as a wisp of drifting cloud to be seen, emphasized the silence and the stillness. The thin blue stream of vapour that slowly trickled from my lungs was the only thing in the world that moved.

I can of course say that it was a strange and unforgettable experience to sit there quite alone looking at the boundless splendour of that mountain landscape. But that doesn't really say much. Those are words which are used every day about things which are straightway forgotten.

If I had had a companion, I suppose I should not have realized how tremendous silence and solitude can be. Even alone, I might not have realized it to the full had not that yellow swine of a driver tipped us over outside Kuldsha and broken my back. I would probably just have filled my lungs, sent an arrogant shout at the hills, and strode off down towards the glacier.

So I sat there telling myself that it was only such and such a distance to Mishgar. But the screes below me looked quite impassable, and suddenly it seemed incredible that there could be other people anywhere in that deathly silent mountain world. There were ominous grumblings coming from my back, and little stabs of fear that it might fail me on what lay ahead mingled with my doubts as to whether it was possible to find a way out of that lifeless wilderness.

I hope the reader will understand me when I say that that was the one and only time in my life I have been alone. Absolutely and bitterly alone. Quite pitiably and completely alone. The silence was immense and absolute, and so oppressive that you felt it physically. The sight of the grim beauty of the Karakorum was impressive beyond belief.

I closed my eyes. The black eyes and unruly forelock of Lakpah Tsjinsjing Sherpa appeared, and his face was like a reflection of the Karakorum—hard, rugged and peculiar, full of mystery:

'Well, now, Sahib Skrede! Are you not altogether pleased with the quietness of Mintaka? Perhaps you would rather have had a little snowstorm with the monsoon whistling through the Pass of a Thousand Ibex. Then, I think, you might have had other things to complain about . . . Oh, no! Sahib, now you are alone before the countenance of the gods. There you will find the truth of what I said about being small. Less than nothing, Sahib. Disappeared. The mountains and the gods alone remain . . .'

But I also saw another pair of eyes: grey-blue like steel, encouraging, calm, unshakable—as our race's will to live —Eric Shipton's eyes:

'Take it easy, Willie,' they said. 'The hut lies just on the edge of the glacier. You must get there before night. The next day ought to take you to Boyhill. From there you'll manage Mishgar in one day. Perhaps you'll meet some Hunzas down in the valley. They are friendly.'

I threw away the stump of my cigarette and began walking.

For the most part the road was not hard to find: scattered heaps of horse droppings, an occasional skeleton, dark-brown splodges of blood from the dripping muzzles of thousands of exhausted horses, stones marked by scrabbling hooves.

Even so there were times when I went wrong. Then I just had to go back and search for horse droppings and spatters of blood.

The hours passed. The road was dreadful in many places, almost to the extent of having to let yourself drop from stone to stone, and at times go on all fours. My rucksack— in which there was not so very much, heaven knows— gradually became incredibly heavy.

I pressed ahead for all I was worth, but that was less than I had realized. My back was painful and I could do nothing about it, but what had happened to my lungs

and legs? Were those my legs which tremblingly protested
against every effort?

I walked and walked. Stumbled and walked on.
Crawled and walked. My tiredness increased progressively.
The screes became worse and worse. Soon I had to rest
every hundred yards. On again. Worse than ever. I had
to edge my rucksack along bit by bit in front of me.

Then it was not far to the glacier.

The sun went down behind the peaks and it became
bitterly cold. The shadows in the ravines grew wider and
wider, crept further and further up. The summits of the
Karakorum glowed like gold, turned violet and then ice-
green. Blasts of cold, black night came up at me with
every step.

It was no longer any use looking for horse droppings or
splodges of blood. It was only skeletons that could show
the way.

Most people don't consider that there's anything nice
about a skeleton, and you would hardly expect one to be an
edifying sight for a lone, hungry and dog-tired poor wretch
stumbling along in the semi-darkness among the boulders
in Mintaka Pass, but whenever I saw a white gleaming
structure of bones in all that blackness, it caused me no
chill of apprehension, but a thrill of joy; 'Keep going,
Willie! You're on the right track.'

Whether the skeleton was of man or beast was all one
to me. Just as long as there were bones . . .

Now I was crawling more than walking. The glacier was
just there . . . but where was the hut?

In the end I felt it hopeless to continue. I crept in
among some great boulders and unrolled my sleeping bag.
While icy night settled over the Karakorum, I slept.

I awoke with a squeezing sensation in my chest and every muscle trembling with cold. My watch showed that I had slept a bare hour.

In the darkness the boulders were like grotesque gnomes, but high above them, above even the great peaks, the stars had sprung forth in the night sky. I had seen them so often in a Norwegian sky, and how badly I wanted once again to see them mirror themselves in a smooth tarn among the woods at home!

No, by all Lakpah's weird divinities, one could become too insignificant!

I realized that I should have to move about and somehow or other keep going among the boulders till morning came. I did knee bends, flapped my arms, and massaged my heart till my blood was circulating again; then I set off once more on my search for the road.

Twenty yards from where I had been lying I found the hut.

It was built between two great boulders and I had to creep on my belly through its little door. Inside I lit a match, closed the apertures a bit better, arranged my sleeping bag and went to sleep again.

I must say that I have spent better nights than that one in the hut by the Mintaka Glacier, and I don't really understand what was wrong with me then. Usually when I lie down to sleep, I do sleep—like a marmot. But there I must have had a touch of mountain sickness and that must take the blame for the unpleasant nightmares which tormented me. I would wake up suddenly, find myself cold and smoke a cigarette or two. Every now and again I would hear a dull boom from the glacier. Whenever I went to sleep again, the nightmares returned.

When daylight came, I crept out. The sky was still without a cloud. My teeth chattered with the cold as I stood there in that chaos of stone and looked up at the peaks bristling towards the heavens.

I crept back into the hut and ate half my biscuits. The daylight filtered through now and I was able to see my way about inside. The only thing to show that people had ever been there was an empty rusty tin.

It was then that I surprised myself.

While I sat there eating my biscuits that empty tin seemed to hypnotize me: corned beef. Corned beef? What in heavens name was corned beef doing in Mintaka?

Suddenly I jumped to my feet, kicked the tin outside, stamped round the hut cursing Quisling and Hitler, then I sat down and laughed aloud.

Equally suddenly I realized that I was being altogether idiotic, that even though I had been exhausted the evening before, there was no reason to behave like that now. I dragged my sleeping bag and the corset outside, drank some of the water that trickled from the glacier and had a smoke. When I tentatively tried my legs I was amazed to discover that I felt in fine fettle.

The way now led along the edge of the glacier—and through the gully to the right of it. Even though it was pretty bad in places, I was making progress. Gradually the gully widened out, the screes became smaller, and after a bit I again found myself in a glen where a stream came stealing out from under the glacier, and gradually grew both big and sprightly.

The sun rose and it became warmer. Small patches of moss were the first welcome signs of returning life. Soon I came across some small stunted bushes that had wedged themselves in among the stones. A vulture was sailing in wide circles round one of the summits.

At midday I found a sort of shed with a slanting roof in front of a slab of rock. Here too I saw some old empty tins to prove that people had been there before me. This time I left them lying.

My rucksack had again become dreadfully heavy, and I rummaged through it to see if there was anything I could discard. But I didn't want to part with any of the things I had there. Some water and a cigarette stilled the clamour of my tummy. I was keeping the biscuits for later. On again.

Further on, I saw a valley beneath me. In one place there below was a little green field ringed by birch woods. That was getting more like it: green pasture, birch woods clambering up the mountainside, distant snow-capped peaks by the dozen behind—it was so familiar and so lovely. The green idyll down there must have been Boyhill. Perhaps I would find people there.

I almost forgot that I was alone. In fine spirits I sat down and gobbled up the remains of my biscuits. Then I had a good smoke before I got going. After that I perked up and sang in my screeching tuneless voice, which did not matter as there was no one to hear me. All the same that hill was horribly long and the going hard, and gradually that dissipated a lot of my good spirits. Then my tiredness returned.

By about four o'clock I had reached the valley, and there I came across a little cabin. There wasn't much to it, but at least it had walls and a roof. There was a hearth and a little cooking place, too, though it was not much use to me as I had no food.

In the hut someone had left a few illustrated magazines as a reminder that civilization did after all exist. Their front pages were covered with pictures of tanks and bombers. From others little cuties with great long eyelashes gazed languishingly at me. I was getting back to civilization all right!

Most of all I wanted to sleep; but I had to content myself with some water and a cigarette and then set off again. The road now became considerably better, and it was pure delight to be able to walk occasionally on grass and banks of moss. Before long I was down at Boyhill and vainly hoping to find somebody. There wasn't a soul to be seen. In the end I caught sight of a couple of camels strolling about among the twisted birches. Where there are camels there must be people too, so I gave vent to a Tarzan howl. No use. Nobody appeared. Nothing happened, except that the camels slowly turned their heads and then resumed their grazing.

After walking round a bit and shouting and kicking up a row, I realized to my disappointment that the camels were the only living beings in Boyhill. It was annoying, but there was nothing to be done about it. By then my rucksack had grown so horribly heavy that I took a rash decision and tipped almost all its contents on a stone and left them there.

It was a good road that led downwards. I was rather angry and that helped too. I went at it hammer and tongs. But my temper of course subsided and I gradually accustomed myself to the idea of a night in the open. I comforted myself with the thought that even though I was still fairly high, it could not be as hellishly cold as on Mintaka. When I considered what Eric Shipton had told me and remembered what I had read in *News from Tartary* I felt that there should be a good chance of meeting people before Mishgar.

When you are trudging along like that, so tired that you feel you could drop where you are, you have to make use of various tricks to keep yourself going. You can, for example, think of something really hard and hellish, and then you forget the struggle and don't notice one foot going in front of the other. If you can manage to sing and bawl a bit, that helps too. If none of those are any good, then there is nothing for it but to try and work yourself up into a rage. When you are in a rage you get along fine.

In the end I managed to make myself pretty furious, and before I knew what was happening I found myself in another little sprinkling of twisted birches and green banks. By then my back was horribly painful and my feet as heavy as lead. I thought that I should park there for the night, and if it were half as cold as on Mintaka I was going to have a bit of a job getting the old mechanism going again in the morning.

Once again I thought I would try a cigarette to pull myself together, and then I heard a sound from among the birches on the slope, a familiar and beloved sound: the dull thud of an axe. What a heavenly sound that was to the ears of a tired tramp at the head of the Hunza valley! For even below Mintaka camels don't cut wood, I told myself. The logical conclusion was that there must be people there.

This time, however, I didn't give a Tarzan shout. I was frightened I might scare the people if I began shouting, so, instead, I walked cautiously towards the sound coming from among the birches, and it was not long before I found a black bearded Hunza busily chopping.

'*Salaam . . . Salaam . . . Salaam aleikom aka,*' I ventured.

The man gave a start, and for a wild moment I was afraid that he would run away—he looked so scared.

Fortunately, he soon pulled himself together, cocked his behind in the air and to my relief replied: '*Salaam aleikom, Sahib!*'

He took the cigarette I proffered and loosed a torrent of words: 'Yes, Sahib! Yes, Sahib!' following every other word. 'Yes' was the only English he knew, and my attempts at Turki remained without effect. When I pointed back and up towards Mintaka and said: 'From Mintaka . . . kik-kik-kikk', and then pointing in the opposite direction: 'To Mishgar', he was on to it at once.

'Yes, Sahib, yes!'

'*Mori? mori?* (Horse)', I asked.

He smiled happily, beamed: 'Yes, Sahib, yes, *mori.*'

It looked as though my troubles were at an end. The man obviously could get me a horse, and perhaps I could get a little food from him too.

He conducted me down through the birch wood to a little stone hut, and there a young boy appeared. Then I achieved something of which I am rather proud, a real feat in fact. Almost exclusively with the help of sign language I managed to make the lad understand that I had left a number of things at Boyhill which I wished him to fetch. The quick-witted lad understood and gave a delighted smile: 'Yes, Sahib!' At that he was off like lightning in the direction of Boyhill, and returned after dark with all my things.

The hut was tiny and tumbledown, but there was a hearth and place for cooking. The man mixed a little flour and water, and baked some bread rather like pancake. Tea and yak's milk they gave me too. It all tasted excellent and I ate a lot. Just before dark a woman appeared with

some yaks. Shortly afterwards the boy returned with my
things, and then we settled down for the night on some rugs
they had laid on the floor of the hut.

Small flames flickered among the remains of the birch
wood on the hearth. Yellow tongues of light licked round
the lumpy figures on the floor and at the rough stones in
the walls. There was the little hut, a few yaks, a horse—
you could be a good bit poorer than that. My three hosts
seemed well pleased with life as they lay there hugging
themselves on the floor beside me. The man and the boy
breathed loudly and regularly. The woman had curled
up and shoved her broad beam against her husband's
belly. There was only a dark red glow left on the hearth.

My back and legs ached so that I felt I wanted to howl
aloud, but I could feel how the yak's milk and the bread
were putting new strength into me. Suddenly I felt a surge
of real affection for that bearded Hunza and his shrivelled
wife and their boy.

What had they done? Nothing but what poor people
living in remote places do almost everywhere: they had
honoured the age-old laws of hospitality.

The Hunza's horse proved to be a very lively stallion. I
had scarcely got my foot in the stirrups before it set off at
a gallop up hill into the birches. I clung on and hauled
at the reins, and eventually the brute had to give in. The
man then took hold of the bridle and led the horse off
down the road. I felt that this was rather a slight: had I
not shown that I could master his old nag? But of course
it was his horse and I could not very well say anything.

Around noon we passed through a narrow glen. At the
foot of a tall cliff, just beside the mouth of the glen, were
a number of Indians building a fort under the supervision

of a native sapper officer. The officer spoke English, and
he told me that he had heard of me, and that a cook, with
all I should need for the trip to Gilgit, would meet me in
Mishgar which was within a mile or two of there.

The cook was the first person we met when we reached
Mishgar. A thin, dark, squat little fellow in a brown shirt,
knickerbockers and high boots. His coal-black, bearded
face was topped by the typical Hunza cap, which is made
of coarse wool and rolled up like a stocking. The whole
appearance of the man inspired confidence. Nor with him
was there any '*Salaam aleikom, Sahib!*' but a smiling:

'Good morning, sir! Mr Skrede?'

Yes, it was.

Slowly and with dignity he produced a letter he had
beneath his shirt, and brought it to me with a certain
ceremony:

'Please, sir.'

It is always nice to get letters, and it was a good time
since I had had one. I studied the typewritten super-
scription:

Mr Wilfred Skrede (Norwegian)
Mishgar

The letter was signed by a Major Crichton of the Gilgit
Scouts. It was a very pleasant letter which told me that
the bearer, Shrukker Ali, would be my cook and boy on
the journey to Gilgit, where there was a room waiting for
me. The Major wished me a pleasant journey . . .

So now I had become a boss!

14. *The Land of the Hunzas*

∧∧∧∧∧∧∧∧∧∧∧∧∧∧∧∧∧∧∧∧∧∧∧∧∧

IN THOSE DAYS a rupee was worth about one shilling and fourpence, and there are sixteen annas to a rupee. I had got a certain amount of Indian money in Kashgar and I gave the Hunza man a few coins in thanks for all his help. I should think it added up to four or five rupees.

At first it looked as though the man didn't understand what I was up to, but when he realized that *he* was to have the money he became almost hysterical, jumping up and down and dancing and crying: 'Sahib, Sahib, Sahib!' Finally he kissed my two hands, leaped into the saddle and tore off down the road in the direction of Mintaka in true Tom Mix style.

Shrukker Ali had watched the scene with an expression of disapproval on his face, and the first thing he did was to give me a lecture in English that was as peculiar as my own.

I must not give those people so much money, I was told. Two or three annas would have been enough. Such people

171

were only accustomed to count in annas and for them a shiny rupee was a fortune. For my part, I told him I was only sorry I had not been able to give the man more. Hadn't they been kind and decent, given me shelter and food, and helped me in every possible way?

'We are in India now,' said Shrukker, 'and a rupee is a lot of money.'

Mishgar is a little village which has attached itself to a grudging stony desert. Tiny stone houses lie surrounded by poplars and apricot trees. Round the houses are small patches of cultivated land arranged in terraces built up with stones. Wooden conduits take water to these fields and the apricot orchards. The whole appearance of the place is one of reasonable prosperity, and yet how meagre and poor it all seemed by comparison with the luxuriant fertility of the oases of Turkestan.

Shrukker conducted me to a little house where we were to spend the night. It was a hut, cosily furnished, and it had a bed which looked most inviting.

Shrukker appeared to be a 'real treasure' and I was glad that I was to have him with me for the rest of my travels through the mountains. In fact, after Mishgar all went swimmingly.

Somehow the knickerbockers Shrukker was wearing seemed strangely familiar. I looked at them more closely: they were *mine*! I could swear that the black little monkey was wearing my well-worn pepper-and-salt knicker-bockers which had been made for me in Oslo and which . . . ?! But how? I come all that long way from Norway, toil laboriously up and across Mintaka Pass—and the first person I meet in India happens to be wearing a pair of my trousers!

'Fine trousers you have, Shrukker!' said I. 'Where can one buy trousers like that?'

The question gave Shrukker an opportunity to tell me what a fine chap he was.

I wasn't to think that this was the first time he had cooked for a Sahib; no, indeed! He had been cook and guide for Sahib this and expedition that. Among others he had earlier that year been guide to three Sahibs who had come travelling across Mintaka Pass. It was one of these, Sahib Sverre, who had given him those splendid trousers, and Sahib Sverre, I was told, 'was a perfect gentleman'.

The explanation was that when the four of us parted company in Kuldsha, our things had got a bit mixed up. My spare trousers had got into Sverre's rucksack and his boots into mine. It was easy to see that the lad had been hard up for cash and so had paid Shrukker for his services with my trousers. I promised myself that when we got safely to Gilgit or Srinagar, Shrukker should have Sverre's boots as well.

Shrukker certainly earned those boots. That very first evening I acquired the greatest respect for his skill as a cook.

With the kindly help of two Indian engineers I found in Mishgar, I concocted a reasonable letter to Eric Shipton, and so, after Shrukker Ali's first wonderful meal, went early to bed tired and exhausted, but full-fed and without a care or worry in the world.

I had scarcely got to sleep when I was awakened by three weird creatures coming into the hut. One held out a bowl with a great lump of butter in it, another proffered a basin of flour, while number three had a sheep on a rope halter. All three cocked their behinds into the air:

'*Baaa, baaa!*' said the sheep.

'*Salaam aleikom, Sahib!*' chanted the three in chorus.

My wits were heavy with sleep and I thought they were trying to sell me the things. I motioned them away:

'No, no, boys . . . I have no money. *Oha, oha . . . Bi jok-jok tenga.*'

But the men persisted. They came nearer the bed and jabbered away all at once. 'Sahib, sahib', was the only word of it I understood. All I wanted was to get rid of them so that I could go back to sleep, but what on earth was I to do? Then Shrukker appeared on the scene and gestured to me that I must take the things:

'Presents to you, Sahib.'

'Presents?'

'Yes, Sahib. From the king . . .'

'? . . . ? . . . ?'

'Yes, Sahib, from Mir Sahib of Hunza.'

Well, I was coming up in the world. Getting presents from kings now! Need I say that I was out of bed in a flash, and then it was my turn to cock my behind in the air. I don't suppose those Hunza boys had ever seen such a queer and grateful Sahib before. With Shrukker's assistance I conveyed a request that they would give my most deferential and respectful thanks to His Highness Mir Sahib.

We made quite a little caravan as we left Mishgar. As well as Shrukker and myself we had a young Hunza boy with us, and the rear was brought up by the sheep, its halter securely tied to the tail of the last horse.

The Gilgit Road can offer you a little of everything in the way of beautiful and impressive scenery. It is also not without its share of creepy and unpleasant traverses and, to enjoy the first day's march out from Mishgar you should not be subject to giddiness.

The road climbed rapidly up the mountainside, twisting and turning from shelf to shelf and couloir to couloir. Soon we could catch a white glimpse of the River Hunza in the black gorge beneath. It was a thousand feet down to it and the face of the mountain was all but perpendicular. On either side of the glen the tops of mountains soared several thousand feet up into the sky. Shrukker and the boy had to heave and pull to get the horses along— riding was out of the question. There was a lot of loose hard rock on the mountainside, and, bursting with pride, Shrukker told me about every one of the fatal accidents that had ever happened there. As though a road like that required extra spicing for the traveller!

Well on in the day we had a descent down to the river so abrupt and precipitous that the horses covered most of it sitting on their backsides. At the bottom was a bridge of rotten timbers strengthened with wire—as though it were playing at being a suspension bridge in its old age. Once safely across we halted for a rest and food.

'Mutton chop, Sahib?' inquired Shrukker pointing at the sheep, and, when I nodded, he unceremoniously knocked it on the head.

The road from there was, if possible, even worse than before. In places iron bolts had been hammered into the rock and some miserable bits of wood laid across them; elsewhere the road had been built up on stones where the mountainside was otherwise too steep, and it looked incredible that those piles of stones could remain in place. I was quite certain that the whole thing must collapse into the gorge the moment people and horses got on it.

In many places it was so narrow that we had to take the baggage off the horses, for it was impossible for them to get along with a pack. Shrukker and the Hunza boy had a stiff job. I was the Sahib and had only myself to see to.

After crossing over yet another strange combination of span and suspension bridge, there came a very steep descent to Gircha, a place of water-conduits and apricot trees, tiny patches of fields and little houses with flat roofs, and all the other things that belong to inhabited places in the land of the Hunzas. There was, though, a comfortable camp-house with a hearth and good equipment and so we stopped for the night.

The people who live in Gircha must be a hard-working and very unpretentious lot, for apart from the man-made toy gardens of their own there wasn't a blade of greenery to be seen. On every side there was naked, crevassed rock, and all round the horizon bunches of sharp inaccessible peaks covered with eternal snow. That little village had a very desolate, cold and inhospitable setting, but it was of course enchantingly beautiful too.

While the industrious Shrukker was busy making our supper of sheep, I sat outside the camp-house and had a smoke. The evening light had turned the steep mountainsides into a flickering sheet of changing colour, and the last of the daylight was making the distant peaks glow like molten copper. The evening shadows went creeping, blue and mysterious, into gorges and couloirs.

The mutton was wonderful. Pleased and happy, I fell asleep for another night in the Karakorum.

After Gircha the road remained as fairy-tale as ever. About noon we reached Chaibar, another little place where the sons and daughters of the Hunza seemed to be hanging on by the skin of their teeth. There, too, was a comfortable camp-house with a hearth and everything in order.

A couple of hours on from Chaibar we came to the great Batura glacier which we had to cross. On the last stretch before the glacier the road was again so steep that the horses nearly tumbled over. Far beneath at the bottom of the dark gorge we could see the river Hunza rushing along in boisterous falls and rapids. Our baggage had to be lashed so that it lay as though stuck to the horses, which had no liking at all for the descent. Shrukker tugged and pulled, and by some means we all got to the bottom.

At the edge of the glacier we found a man with a yak-ox. Shrukker told me that Mir Sahib had ordered it to be there, for he knew that the foreign Sahib had injured his back and the yak was to save him the hardship of the glacier. On the yak's broad back was a saddle laid over a wad of colourful rugs and placed well behind the small of its back. On this I sat in the utmost comfort.

At the edge of the glacier the greeny-blue ice was dirty with earth and gravel. Stones and points of rock stuck up through it, and there were clutching tentacles of dirty-grey ice hanging down the sides of the gorge towards the river.

The passage of the Batura glacier was hard work for Shrukker and the Hunza boy, to say nothing of the poor horses. They were continually toppling over, legs flying and kicking to get a hold. At a number of points their packs had to be taken off and carried. But how different for Sahib Skrede! The Hunza walked ahead with thick socks over his boots leading the ox by a ring in its nose. The old yak plodded along as sedate and staid as a bridegroom in church. Whenever there was a bit of a downward slope, it just subsided on its behind and slid.

Yak-ox means grunting ox and, true enough, when we were safely across the glacier and I went up to the kindly brute that had taken me over and scratched it between the horns as a way of saying thank you, it really did grunt like a contented pig.

That Mir Sahib who had shown such thought and consideration for an unknown vagabond who came tramping into his mountain realm must, I felt, be a remarkable potentate.

From there to Passo the road was level and good. In one place it was even so good that I was able to try a bit of a gallop. At Passo I was back in the world of poplars and mud houses. The hut in which we spent the night was excellent and Mir Sahib's sheep reappeared in a new and even more delicious form.

We started out from Passo early in the morning so as to be able to reach Baltit in good time that evening. Baltit is where Mir Sahib resides and Shrukker told me that his guest house was all ready to receive us. Mir Sahib was expecting us to spend a quiet day or two there.

We had a short midday halt in the lovely village of Gulmit which was slightly larger than the other places we had come through. Mir Sahib had a place there where he stayed for part of the year.

Just before we reached Sarat, we saw the stone monument Mir Sahib put up in memory of Lord Kitchener who once paid him a visit. Apparently the two of them got on well together.

Our next halt was in Altit, a sort of suburb to Baltit. It is perhaps the loveliest of all the small villages of the Hunza country. A long narrow lake at the bottom of a deep glen surrounded with poplars, and a picturesque little old fortress perched on a crag, and behind it Rakaposhi, over 25,000 feet high, monumental and mighty in all its lovely inaccessible whiteness.

For the last stretch along the Hunza river we again had to creep along narrow shelves in the mountainsides. In places you looked straight up at the overhanging rock. Where there was a bend in the valley we saw Baltit beneath us with the Mir's castle standing erect and resplendent on a spur on the west side of the valley. We crossed the river just above the dams that supply the town's irrigation system.

Down in the valley stood a large tent in a garden among great fruit trees, and there I was quartered. It contained the bed of all time, and there too I found wash-stands and toilet things and at once set about spring-cleaning myself. I hadn't had a decent wash since Kashgar and looked like it.

Clean and freshly shaven, I stood outside the tent smoking a cigarette. Peace and quiet lay over the Mir's town, and all at once I found myself humming a tune about the beauties of the evening sun.

Had I ever seen the evening sun so bewitchingly beautiful as there in Baltit? A swishing murmur from the Hunza river came stealing through the apricot trees.

Some chap with most phenomenal lungs began bawling from somewhere beyond the town:

'*Allah! Allah akbar! Allah! Allah! Allah Akbaaaar!*'

And then it broke out everywhere: '*Allah akbar. Allah akbar!*'

On the other side of the trees in the garden someone joined in the chorus, and going to look I saw Shrukker Ali and one or two others lying flat on their faces with arms outstretched. As I stood there smoking, I realized that at that moment I was the only person in Baltit on his feet. Everybody from those in the mud houses to Mir Sahib himself, every single one of them would be flat on his face with his head in the direction of Mecca.

'*Allah! Allah akbar!*'

I felt myself a heathen among the faithful, yet even though I were an infidel—a *kafir*—and a stranger among the men of Hunza, I was by no means a damned dog of a *parang*, suspect pig of an Anglee spy, as I had been in Turkestan where one and all spat at me. Here, in fact, I was the Sahib. Shrukker Ali was my boy and good fairy and Mir Sahib himself my high protector.

There were a number of little houses in the orchard. In one of these my dinner was served. The room was large and comfortable: great fireplace, thick soft rugs, heavy carved furniture, a table laden with a large selection of cigars, cigarettes and magazines, and a deep armchair. From one of the beams in the roof hung an enormous candelabra with candles in it.

Shrukker Ali withdrew and left it to one of the Mir's servants to see to my wellbeing. The tall dark Hunza made a magnificent figure in his white clothes with a broad blue silk sash round his waist, which was fastened with a huge clasp that appeared to be silver. He bowed and scraped to me as though I had been a Mir myself.

The cooking was European and the food really excellent. There was rice, meat and vegetables, and at the end a heavenly dessert of mixed fruit.

You may well imagine that I was on top of the world when, the meal over, I settled myself in one of the deep chairs, crossed my legs and planted a huge cigar in one corner of my mouth.

I was the Sahib all right!

As I sat there looking through the magazines and blowing clouds of smoke at the brown beams in the roof, I thought of how life does take you up and down. Then Shrukker appeared and said that Mir Sahib's son, Mir Junior, had come to call.

Junior was a man of medium height in his thirties. His smiling face was perhaps a shade lighter than the skins of most Hunzas. His eyes were large and shining, and he had a little black beard and a suit of English tweed and excellent cut which at once made me very wobbly in my new-found dignity as a sahib. In fluent English he bade me welcome to Baltit, brought me greetings from Mir Sahib himself, and said that his father hoped I would rest at Baltit for a few days as his guest. As I sat desperately racking my brains for adequate English words I once again felt the poor bemused tramp. It made me feel slightly better, though, when Junior said that his father was looking forward to meeting what he called 'this Northern Columbus', which he hoped would be at the castle for lunch the following day.

Mir Junior was a princely person—there was no getting away from that. Besides he had spent several years at Oxford and was a complete man of the world. That was more than could be said of me, so it is no wonder I felt a little awkward. But he was awfully nice and I soon pulled myself together and thanked him more or less decently for all their kindness. Then we talked a bit together—mostly about my journey—and so His Highness said goodnight and withdrew.

I must admit that I didn't get to sleep at once. Perhaps it was too much of a good thing having an eiderdown again, for many a time I had fallen asleep instantly on a

hard mud bunk. Perhaps it was the thoughts which inevitably came which kept me awake. Away in the north
perhaps someone was wondering where Willie might be
at that moment—and there he was cudgelling his poor
brains over how to behave with princes and kings!

'How do you do, Mir Sahib . . .' Good God, I couldn't
say that!

'Your Majesty . . . your Royal Highness . . .'

Did I say Columbus?

Sahib Skrede had stage-fright.

Less than twenty thousand people live in Mir Sahib's
country, and not many more could feed themselves in
that extensive but infertile land. There is no agriculture
other than the small cultivated patches that have been
scraped out of the gullies and ravines, and even these are
only to be found where it is possible to install a system of
irrigation. Nor can there be much of a pastoral industry,
for the mountains and uplands are too rough and sterile.
Here and there, however, there is a little grass for the
yaks, corn grows in the tiny fields round the villages, and
in every gully where it is at all possible they have planted
golden apricots. Even so it is difficult to understand how
the people can scrape along. Frugal their tastes have to be.

This wild country with all its towering mountain peaks
has bred a proud and handsome people. Most of the men
are slim and well-proportioned, and their carriage is as
limber and supple as an animal's. The usual dress is
trousers and tunic of white linen. If it is cold they put on
a long-sleeved caftan of winsey-like woollen material on
top. On their feet they have *coplis*, brown shoes like sandals
having sharp iron brads on the sole.

Some of the women I saw were so lovely, both of body

and face, that you would not see any to beat them in the September evening parades along Karl Johans Street in Oslo—or anywhere else for that matter. Nowhere between Shimpanse and Bombay did I see such healthy, well clad and clean kids as in Baltit. And they looked happy, too.

When I was among the wary, scowling Turkis, from whom you could never get a straight answer and who always did their best to find something other than the truth to tell you, I always had the feeling of being a *parang*, an Anglee who was not welcome. In Baltit, or anywhere else in the country of the Hunzas, people looked you in the face and you had the feeling of being among friends.

There are many stories about the fight this mountain people made to preserve its independence. When in the end, peace returned to the mountains, the poor Hunza lands had come under the control of the Government of India. Mir Sahib has been his people's overlord for over half a century and in that time has made himself loved, and acquired a reputation for ruling his people well and wisely.

Baltit, the capital, lies in a basin where there is a bend in the valley. On the valley floor are orchards and up the slopes are mud houses arranged in terraces and surrounded by poplars and apricot trees. High up, on a flat spur above the town, is the Mir's castle, shining white against the black rock. Many thousands of feet above, the summits of the mountains end in everlasting snow. They are not dwarfs, the ones which stand guard over Mir Sahib's town: Dhasto Ghil, a little to the east of Baltit, is close on 26,000 feet. And it was up in that white castle that Sahib Skrede, alias the Northern Columbus, stood waiting for his lunch.

It had been a busy morning. We had set about our

preparations immediately after an excellent breakfast. My riding breeches were brushed and rubbed and sponged. Shrukker rubbed my boots with fat and polished them till he was blue in the face. He kept holding them up, for he wished to mirror himself in them, but never were they shiny enough, then he would call upon Allah, tear his hair and have a go at them again. In the end they were as glossy as patent leather.

I had a red-checked sports shirt which I thought was just the right thing, but Shrukker resolutely refused to accept it. No, he would rather take a trip to the bazaar and see if he could find his Sahib a decent shirt there. Then I fished out of my rucksack Tanja's white linen shirt with the blue embroidery, and that was considered satisfactory. When Shrukker made his final inspection, he smiled a satisfied smile:

'Okay Sahib!'

It was obvious that he loved his Mir and badly wanted the strange Sahib to make a good impression.

When the time arrived a whole delegation came to fetch us. Shrukker was unable to restrain himself and at the last moment he bustled off with my boots to give them one last polish. Then we walked in dignified procession up the steep zigzags to the castle. Everyone we met stopped and bowed: '*Salaam aleikom, Sahib!*'

When we reached the lowest of the castle's terraces we passed through a carved wooden gateway and into a large hall, and from there up some steep steps the last of which led through an opening in the roof. From there I had to go on alone. The delegation came to a solemn halt, and Shrukker nearly had tears in his eyes as he called out:

'Good luck, Sahib!'

Up on the flat terrace stood a line of white-clad servants.

Beyond, at the entrance to the castle proper, stood the Mir and his son waiting. I felt slightly nervous as I walked across towards them, but when the servants bowed and sang out '*Salaam aleikom, Sahib*', I had sufficient presence of mind left to fling out one arm and reply '*Salaam aleikom!*'

Mir Mohammed Nazim Khan was a magnificent old man with a lot of beard and wise gentle eyes. His foot-length, wine-red tunic was edged with broad silver-embroidered ribbon all down from the neck to the hem. He wore a turban on his head. Junior was in tweeds, as he had been the day before.

I have no proper recollection of how I got through the initial formalities, and I am afraid that I did not show up very well. But the prince was kindness itself and gave my hand a long and cordial shake before conducting me into the castle proper.

First we entered a great hall with chairs and carved chests along the walls on which hung hunting trophies: heads of ibex and other game, and a collection of arms and weapons. There were, too, a number of photographs, among them one of Lord Kitchener. Then we went into the Mir's drawing-room. This was not so big, but richly furnished with colourful carpets and cushions. Mir Sahib seated himself in a large armchair and Junior and I sat down on either side of him. The chairs were placed in an embrasure in one wall where there were windows on three sides with leaded panes and small glass paintings.

Unfortunately I have not been entertained by other princes, so I am unable to make comparisons. I imagine that Mir Mohammed Nazim Kahn has many colleagues up and down the world who have more palatial dwellings, but I doubt if any has such a beautiful view from his audience chamber. It would not be easy to find a lovelier mountain panorama than that on which we looked, and beneath us lay the town. We looked right down on to the flat roofs of its houses and to the many poplars. Through the tops of trees farther into the valley we could catch glimpses of the river, like snippets of silver wire.

A servant served whisky and soda. On the table were cigars and English cigarettes. I could not very well ask why neither of my princely hosts either smoked or drank, but, repeating an experiment made in Kashgar, I discovered once again that what comes from Scotland is good. I think it was Red Label.

The Mir himself spoke no English, but we chatted with his son as interpreter. Rather stammeringly I thanked them for the wonderful reception I had had, and for the gifts. I assured them that their country had made an unforgettable impression on me—and that was fully in accordance with the truth. I went on to say that I myself came from a land of mountains, though the mountains there were more modest than theirs, and that my country had been attacked by bandits and my King had had to leave it. I was on my way to join him and do what I could to help him drive the swine out. Junior translated, then, smiling, he told me that his father was aware of Norway's fate and the fight being made by the Norwegians, and that they both admired King Haakon for his noble conduct.

Then I had to tell them about the adventures of my journey, and even though my abilities as a teller of tales were inadequate, I was glad that I had something to relate which could interest a majesty. Afterwards Mir Sahib asked me a lot of questions about various conditions in Europe, questions of a kind which showed that if anyone needed putting in the picture it was I and not my hosts. I had to think hard to avoid making a fool of myself.

It became time to eat. The dining-room was adjacent. I was put at the end of a long table with one of my princely hosts on either side. There was, however, only one cover laid and to find that I alone was going to eat while two princes sat and watched, was almost too much of a good thing. I supposed I looked like on outsize mark of interrogation, for Junior told me that neither he nor his father could keep me company as that was a period of fasting and they begged to be excused. Their religion forbade them to partake of food or drink between sunrise and sunset.

That was the first and only time I have eaten at a table where the service was all of heavy, gleaming silver, but, to be truthful, I have often eaten food that I liked better. Something, perhaps mere etiquette, required that in the Mir's house I must eat true Indian food, and the multiplicity of dishes were so highly spiced that I repeatedly thanked heaven for the fact that there was water on the table with which I could assuage my burning throat. I consider it rather an achievement that I got through that meal without displaying an impolite lack of appetite.

After lunch there were more drinks. Mir Sahib was the perfect host. They even went so far in honour of the poor 'Northern Columbus' as to put on a show of dancing for him in the garden. Two or three chaps sat twanging on stringed instruments while some young boy in colourful kaftans danced. I clapped my hands energetically after each number, sincerely hoping that clapping was considered a sign of enthusiasm in Baltit. To be truthful I did not understand anything of it. The dancing for the most part consisted of the boys walking round and round with stiff legs waving their arms so that the long sleeve of their kaftans swayed and swung this way and that.

I spent a number of very pleasant hours there, but in

the end I had to say thank you and goodbye. However, I was not allowed to go until Mir Sahib had taken me to a store and produced some gifts. I became the happy owner of an embroidered kaftan, some Hunza caps, two pairs of coplis and a pair of embroidered slippers. I was really touched by all their kindness and thanked them as well as I could. The Mir wished me good luck on my further journey.

'It has cost you a deal of hardship to come out to me,' said he. And I can still remember the expression there was in the eyes behind those gold-rimmed spectacles, when he added: 'But freedom is worth a little hardship.'

Before I left Baltit the following day I received one further proof of the Mir's thoughtfulness: a lad came leading a horse which was to remain at my disposal until I reached Gilgit. I don't believe Sigurd Jorsalfar can have been more proud when he rode into Miklagaard, than I was as I rode through the Mir's park and out through Baltit on that horse with its tassels and its ribbons braided in mane and tail.

There is not much to relate about the journey from Baltit to Gilgit. The road was good all the way and the Mir's horse a fine one. We rode hard the whole day, paused for lunch at Minapir and after a rest and some tea by the ruins of an old fort, we reached Cholt in the evening. From my diary I see that in Cholt I made myself comfortable in a good chair on the veranda of the guest house and that I had fruit and a bottle of wine—who sent me those?

The following day Shrukker and I rode away from the Hunzas leaving them to come on with our baggage, and so we reached Gilgit when it was still early afternoon.

That was quite a fast stage, but for one reason or another I had a fit of impatience and was in a hurry to be on, so for long stretches at a time we went at a gallop. Shrukker Ali had his hands full to keep up with me and he protested energetically, but in vain. The people of the caravans and others we met just gaped when they saw the crazy Sahib thunder past.

Where the Hunza valley meets the Gilgit valley the road takes a swing round a ridge and after that is almost flat right into Gilgit. Those last few miles we covered pretty fast. The road ran past a temporary aerodrome and then crossed the Gilgit river on a huge long suspension bridge, on the other side of which were bazaars and swarming life, and there was no lack of poplars there either.

When we reached the gateway into Agency House in Gilgit, I saw a number of white women and men standing on a lawn inside and I imagined that I could just barge right in. But Sahib or not the sentry stopped me and I had to ride in the back way. Not till then, when I had jumped down, did I realize that I had ridden harder than was right for the horse's sake and Major Crichton would not have been a true Englishman if he had not given me a sound ticking off for the lather on my horse. Shrukker came in for some of it too, and he explained miserably that he had done his best to make me slow down but that Sahib Skrede had suddenly gone quite crazy.

'Well . . .' said the Major and at once was friendly and amiable again. He was astonished, however, that we had come from Baltit in just a little over a day and a half. Normally it took three days.

The company on the lawn were rather wondering who the man was standing there in a corset, and when they were told that it was Mr Skrede, the Norwegian they were expecting, there was quite a commotion.

Gilgit boasted of a temporary aerodrome, but otherwise that little town in the plain between the mountains was a godforsaken spot. It is a ten or twelve days' journey on horseback from there to Srinagar. The road goes across the Burzil Pass, among others, which though not one of the worst in the Himalayas, is quite high enough and has so much snow that Gilgit is to all intents and purposes cut off from the outside world for half of every year.

Many of the British officers serving in Gilgit had their families with them, and to look at those people you would never imagine you were in one of the hidden-away places of the world. Out there in the wilds they stuck to the formalities and dressed for dinner every evening. On their bridge evenings or at their cocktail parties you might have thought yourself transported to what I imagine London used to be, for all the men were in dinner jackets and the ladies in evening dresses.

It is, in fact, the women one must admire most, the wives who had gone with their husbands to the wilds of the Himalayas. They were pretty fine representatives of their country.

After I had paid a visit to the barber and had my appearance attended to, I went up to the hospital where my back was x-rayed and examined thoroughly. It was rather different there to what I had experienced in Kuldsha: the sick of Hunza and Nagar were accommodated there in beds with gleaming white sheets and everything was neat and sanitary.

We remained four days in Gilgit during which I stayed with the hospitable kindly Crichtons. I had a fine room with a bath, but it took me a little while to get accustomed

to all the Indian servants who stood everywhere and
bowed whenever you passed. Shrukker followed me like a
shadow. His Sahib's things must always be in order.

I went to a tailor and had a light khaki suit made and
that too improved my appearance. Whenever I approached the gateway all the men of the guard came
running out, fell into line and stood stiffly at attention.
Oh yes! Mr Skrede was still the Sahib!

The very first evening I landed in a large house-
warming party given by one of the officers, Captain
Sandy. Everyone else wore a dinner jacket, and I was in
riding breeches and boots, but it didn't matter.

Miss Montgomery, who was the schoolmistress, took
charge of me and showed me the sights of Gilgit. They
were perhaps not very remarkable, but they were impressive in their own way. For example, there was a
monster of an old gun which the Hunzas had used in their
brave but hopeless fight for freedom. The curious thing
about it is that they brought it from Yarkand in Sinkiang.
It sounds incredible, but somehow or other they lugged it
across the mountains. And what would you say to a
caterpillar-car set up as a monument? Believe it or not,
but the Gilgit Road was once covered by a caterpillar-car
from Srinagar to Kashgar. Of course, it required several
hundred coolies, horses and camels as well. It was only
now and then that the car was assembled and driven, but
for most of the way it had to be carried in bits. I bet the
cost per mile of that journey was fairly high, and that it
will be some time before it is done again! But of course
advertisement means a lot.

The others apparently had spent a week in Gilgit and
according to what I was told they were then most likely
still in Bombay waiting with other Norwegians for a boat

to England. I tried sending a telegram to Andrew care of the Norwegian Consulate, but there was no reply.

Ramadan, the month of fasting, ended while I was in Gilgit. The last day of Ramadan is a great festival, for it is then that the followers of Mohammed make up for a month's lost time. From early morning Mohammedans from all the hill places for many miles around came streaming into Gilgit: men, women and children. What a diversity of colours in their kaftans, shawls and turbans! The first item on the day's official programme was a polo match between the British officers and the natives. The polo ground was the size of a football ground and was beautifully situated with avenues of stately poplars down either side. On one side was a stand with reserved seats for the British and more eminent natives—and there was one for Sahib Skrede too. Behind it was a bandstand and a band that played throughout the entire match making an appalling row.

It was a nerve-racking performance. In my own mind I was convinced that somewhere behind the scenes there must have been a staff of doctors and veterinary surgeons in readiness. Those British officers certainly knew how to manage a horse, and it was they who won—but the Hunza lads were not far behind them.

After that there was a mounted shooting match. Using a flying start the competitors came up the ground at a gallop and just as they passed the stand fired at targets put up on the opposite side. The British won that as well.

All day the streets of the bazaar were crowded with people and lively with buffoonery; but we went home and refreshed ourselves with a good whisky and soda and took things quietly till the dance festival began in the evening. It was dark then and the open space was illuminated with

great bonfires. There were no native women to be seen,
for among the Mohammedans it is the men who have all
the say in everything. They keep their women very much
in order, and when the feast of Ramadan reaches its
climax the women, thank you, must toddle off home.

For once Sahib Skrede was not conspicuous. He wore
all his finery: Hunza cap, Mir Sahib's embroidered kaftan
and coplis.

The morning's concert from the bandstand was like a
mumbled prayer compared with the ear-splitting hullabaloo that broke out that evening. The singing and
dancing were on a par with the music. I have no doubt
that there is something very fine about that Mohammedan
so-called folk dancing, but it is queer when you don't
understand it, and to me it was pure savagery. The yells
grew wilder and wilder, the gestures of the dancers more
and more grotesque, and the orchestra blazed away.

But, while Allah's children surrendered to ecstasy,
Sahib Skrede wandered off home to his good bed, for the
following day he was to start on the last stage of his
journey through the Himalayas. Shrukker Ali and he still
had ten days in the hills ahead of them.

15. The Oread of Bandipur

NOT FAR TO the east of Gilgit the two rivers Hunza and Gilgit meet, and a little farther to the east—just before Bunz—those rampageous daughters of the Karakorum join forces with the Indus which rises away on the plains by Yumba Matsen in Tibet, near Lakpah's sacred mountain, Kailas. On its long way westward through the valleys of the Himalayas, the Indus grows large and mighty. At Bunz it finds an opening to the south, squeezes through the mountains, flows through Kohistan, reaches the plains of the Punjab and begins its long journey across the lowlands of India until it finally reaches the sea east of Karachi.

We rode down an open valley. The road ran along the west side of the river. It was a melancholy, desolate valley where sand, gravel, stones and rock were about all you saw. Only along the fringe of the river did a little scrub and grass grow. Relatively seldom did we see any horses or cows, or a solitary camel, searching for a few blades of grass. Occasionally there was a place where man had

made himself a little plot to cultivate with the assistance
of an irrigation system.

A lot of work has been put into the road between
Gilgit and Srinagar, and for riding it is first-class. Long
stretches of it have been cut out of the sandstone. In
places, I suppose, it can be a bit uncomfortable to traverse
if you are not good at heights, but it is not in any way
comparable to the Jacob's ladder up from Mishgar.

At first we had the company of one of the Gilgit officers,
Captain James, who was going up into the mountains on
duty. At the comfortable camp-house in Pari he gave us
a magnificent dinner with whisky and soda and other
good things. The following day we parted company ten
miles farther down the road. We crossed the Indus by a
wooden bridge and continued up to the pleasant little
village of Bunz which is beautifully sited on a crag with
poplars and cultivated land around it.

After Bunz the road was difficult in parts and the slopes
pretty dangerous. On the ascent to the Astor Pass we
crossed a bridge of impressively daring construction across
a perpendicular gorge. We then had Nanga Parbat ahead
of us. That 26,000-foot giant with its magnificent profile
against a blue sky was a bewitching sight. I am not surprised that so many Himalayan climbers have dreamed
of getting to its top. Didn't a German expedition come to
a tragic end there some years before the war?

In the Astor Pass I renewed acquaintance with real cold.
Once across it we came down into fir woods where the
road was good. I rode along a little ahead of the others
and on turning a sharp bend, I suddenly encountered a
woman on a horse. She gave a scream, leaped off her
horse and ran into a cleft in the rock and hid there while
she desperately tried to get the veil over her face. It was

a lovely face and obviously she did not show it to all and sundry.

The following day we crossed the Burzil Pass. It was cold but brilliantly sunny, and we had a heavenly ride. The pass lies 13,000 feet above sea level. There was a little snow up there, and it was almost comical to see how they had built a little hut on stakes thirty or forty feet high. The snow drifts can be enormous, and the hut was for the use of those who have the rather unenviable job of carrying the post for Gilgit. At that time there were only tiny drifts at the bottom of the pass—and there were green patches of ice on some little tarns.

After Burzil were fir-woods again, then we came to an idyllic place called Pehswari where we rested in a delightful mountain hut.

The next place was Gurez, and it was obvious that we were getting out of the wilderness. There was a large inn and a post office, and even something in the nature of a general store. Shrukker promised that by the next evening we should be in Bandipur from which, he said, there was a motor road to Srinagar.

Since crossing the Astor Pass I had seen many spots that reminded me of Norway. We had ridden along slopes wooded with scattered fir-trees and clumps of birches bowed by the mountain winds; places where the roots of fallen trees had peeled off earth's covering and the trees themselves were lying with bristling branches, and those too were a familiar homely sight. When we had surmounted the last of the passes, Traghal Pass, where we met an Englishman who was on his way out fishing, and had reached a bluff from which we could see Bandipur down in a green valley, the resemblance to Norway was so strong that a lump came into my throat.

We had time and to spare so I said to Shrukker that we must stop for five minutes, for I wanted to go off by myself for a bit.

'Okay,' said Shrukker. He would take the opportunity to prepare a meal.

So I rode along the mountainside. Before long I dismounted and walked on, wading through autumnally brown heather which here and there had assumed a hectic cinnabar red, crossed a stream that gurgled past fallow tussocks, and scraped my boots on silver-grey moss growing fell and stone.

Ye gods, exactly the same as at home!

I sat down by a little blinking pool, on the other side of which was a crag with some purple and pink splodges in the cracks, and the whole was mirrored in the water along with small tufts of cloud.

'Yee-hee-hee!' whinnied a horse somewhere quite close, and my tired pony flung up his shaggy head and answered.

I looked up and on a small mound close beside me was a fine girl on a horse. The fair sex has discovered many attitudes to set off its beauty, but a girl can never make a stronger impression than when seen from slightly below while sitting on a thoroughbred which is pricking its ears and arching its neck in a curve of wild strength. The specimen sitting on that magnificent horse—beige riding breeches and white blouse, and brown hair streaming in the wind—was enough to bowl anyone over.

Shrukker and I had been a good many days in the hills and I had been a bit casual about shaving and such like, so it was no wonder that she frowned slightly.

Eventually I managed to produce a husky 'how do you do?'

She bent very slightly forward over her horse's neck:

'Where in heaven's name do you come from?'

'Norway.'

'Norway?' She was puzzled.

By now I had pulled myself together and thought it was time to assert myself.

'Yes, from Norway. Through Russia, Chinese Tartary, Sarikol and Mintaka.'

'From Norway!' she reiterated in amazement.

In the end I had to go off with her to a hut she had nearby and give a more detailed account of how I came to be in Bandipur, and thus it was with a rather bad conscience that I returned to Shrukker Ali a couple of hours later. Poor chap, he must have been afraid he was going to lose his precious Sahib just at the last moment. But Shrukker merely asked why I had not invited the Mem-sahib to eat with us. That was the custom and good manners in that part of the world, said he.

We sat there looking out over the valley of Kashmir. The motor-road wound like a light grey pack-thread through the valley and up to Bandipur. Here I gave Shrukker Sverre's boots as a token of friendship. They were darned fine boots, too. He was going with me to Bandipur, of course, it was just that . . . well, we had met in the mountains and become friends there, and I thought that we ought to say our goodbyes up there as well.

Shrukker was a grand little chap, and my vagabond's heart glowed with pleasure when I saw how happy he was as he pulled on his boots and took a few trial steps in them along the mountainside. He was not only a good cook and a good guide, he had also become a friend. I sincerely hope that when he explained to others where he got his fine boots from, he was able to tell them that Sahib Skrede was 'a perfect gentleman'.

So there beneath us lay Bandipur and the motor road to Srinagar; and in Srinagar there were hotels, theatres, white people and everything you could want—in other words civilization.

From Srinagar was a motor-road to Rawalpindi and from there a railway ran to the cities by the sea, to Norwegian boats.

It was in a strange frame of mind that I sat smoking a last cigarette before we made our way down.

Of course I was glad. For six months I had longed for that moment day and night. At times I had thought that I should never live to experience it. We human beings are strange creatures, however, and much as I had longed for just this very thing it was not without a pang of sadness that I sat and remembered many things: days and nights in Takla Makan, the caravanserais, the *guristans* with their bones and skulls, the swarms in the bazaars, the enchanting loveliness of Rakaposhi and Nanga Parbat— were those all things I should never experience again? Done with?

Even that night in the Pass of a Thousand Ibex was wonderful now that it was but a memory.

But my golden-brown oread had said that in Srinagar we should meet again.

16. Paradise on Earth

ONE DAY I suppose I will become sensible and then I shall set about making money. I shall scrape and save and be mean and miserly until I think I have enough. And I know exactly what I shall do then.

I shall go to Srinagar.

I shall get myself a houseboat.

One like that Dutchman had, where we went for that cocktail party. With many rooms luxuriously furnished; green marble bath and a garden on the roof.

I shall sit among roses on the roof-garden and think back to the days when I was poor and had to work for my daily bread and lived in a queer country far to the north where there was more rain than sunshine.

Perhaps I shall have a whisky and soda to sip at and blow blue cigar smoke up towards the green tops of the chinear trees. The scent of rose and lotus, rhododendron and orchid will confuse my senses, and the Indian sun and a cool breeze from Jhelum compete to increase my physical well-being.

I shall be able to look across the almond and mango trees growing beside the canal where my houseboat is anchored and see gleaming Srinagar—look beyond the wooded slopes, the colourful riot of the heath round Bandipur as far as snow-white Hamarukh shutting out any further view towards Burzil and Nanga Parbat. The giants of the Himalayas in their white turbans will be lined up as a guard of honour for the queen of Kashmir.

And when I have looked my fill at the beauty of the vale of Kashmir and feel that I need a little exercise, I will take a car and drive up to Bandipur; I will go up to the snow, put on a pair of skis, tear off my shirt and while I glide over the snows of India its sun will gladden my heart and warm me through and through. Then on with windproofs and far up the mountain to test the muscles of my legs in a real downhill spin.

The day after that I shall take a trip down along Jhelum. There I shall tease the monkeys which make such a racket in the woods. I shall pick oranges and figs and pineapples and take them home.

Perhaps I shall potter about the woods with a gun. What should I choose: birds, hares or foxes? Perhaps tiger . . .

Perhaps I shall go along the river fishing. Even though, in the eyes of the English, that is no fun as there are far too many fish.

Perhaps one evening I shall toss up to decide whether to go to a garden party and see the women of Srinagar blossom in all their glory, or spend it at the feet of an old yogi . . .

That's the sort of life you can lead in Srinagar if you have enough cash. In Srinagar which lies on the golden mean between the eternal mortal cold of the High Himalayas and the dancing heat of the plains.

There I will forget that there is another world which is governed by suspicion and envy, where stupid people squabble for power and wealth, and ruin life for each other.

It's where Adam and Eve lived in their day, and if anyone tries to tell you that their famous paradise lay somewhere between the Tigris and Euphrates, you can tell them from me that there must be some mistake. Paradise can have been only at Srinagar, in the valley of Kashmir, the most wonderful of all lovely valleys of the world.

However, the road from paradise to hell is never long, and nowhere shorter than in the Srinagar of my day. White, yellow and dark-brown millionaires vied with each other over the luxury of their palaces. Ragged, wretched creatures crept into miserable huts made up of reeds—and were glad to do so. There were plenty who were stark naked and had to lie down in the street when they must sleep. Shiny motorcars slid noiselessly down the avenues. Maharajahs walked about in tunics each of which had cost a fortune; yet the scabby donkey-drivers had merely a tattered piece of cotton round their loins. A pedestrian would soon have been halted unless he knew the correct Anglo-Indian oaths with which to force himself a passage through the stinking horde of dirty, emaciated beggars swarming round him crying: '*Baksheesh, sahib! Baksheesh, sahib!*'

The best hotels in Srinagar were filled with rich people from all over the world, and you didn't dare put your nose inside at night unless you were in evening dress. Not far away in a hovel there would be a poor devil asleep on a mud bunk for which he had paid an anna.

Oh, yes, there were differences indeed in neighbourhood and prices. There were strange beings who for an anna or two offered to sell their daughters of ten or twelve;

while in a certain establishment discreetly situated between a rajah's palace and a millionaire's luxurious villa, you paid ten rupees for a drink and there you could sip of the delights of love for another hundred rupees.

Rats, dogs and emaciated children fought for the scraps on the rubbish-heaps of Srinagar. A few thousand people lived lives of luxury. Many more thousands died every year of tuberculosis, typhus and starvation. Both luxury and misery existed side by side in the fairy-tale beauty of the land of Kashmir. For the few days I was in Srinagar, however, I was on the paradise side and it was only occasionally I found the door ajar and my horrified eyes looked into hell.

One day my oread from Bandipur and I were sitting beneath an awning in the stern of a long and dainty river boat, while the shikari boys paddled us through one of the innumerable canals of Srinagar. The boat slid slowly across the calm surface of the water, the blades of the paddles occasionally brushed a lotus flower, the air was pure and clear, and to the south the white lances of Pir Panjal shone against the blue and cloudless sky. Gently we dipped out into one of the lakes formed by the Jhelum.

Some people call Srinagar the Venice of the East. I have never been to Venice, and I don't suppose I shall ever get there, but I have read books about it and its gondolas and tinkling mandolines beneath a large golden moon. Above Jhelum was no seductive moon, but bright sunshine, and if I had had a mandoline I imagine my oread would have jumped in and swum away from me.

As we sat there side by side I knew that I was going to get quite better and that life was rather wonderful. We looked into each other's eyes, she smiled and showed some gleaming teeth in a golden-brown face.

It was as one might expect and it ended in a scandal. Here is the tale of our fall from grace.

Up from behind us came another boat, much bigger, much more magnificent and with many sweating shikari boys to paddle it. The whole boat was a mass of silks and tassels and frippery, and on something rather like a throne sat a glistening fat rajah or maharajah—which I didn't know—looking down with infinite disdain at the world around him. At the sight of him a devil entered into me and I said to my oread:

'We must race him. Get the boys to paddle harder.'

My oread was on them at once:

'Hurry up, hurry up!'

The boys' black faces twisted wryly, but what the Mem-sahib had said was law. Yet however hard they paddled, the other boat drew gradually but relentlessly away from us. I seized an oar and paddled for all I was worth. That helped, but it was not enough. My oread would not have been the grand girl she was if she could have resisted the temptation to seize an oar herself. Her training did the trick: foot by foot we caught the other boat up, drew level, passed it.

Then my oread and I dropped our oars and burst into peals of laughter.

But there was all the contempt in the world in the eyes of the fat Indian, and we realized that we had committed an awful *faux pas*. Paddling was just work for boys, wretchedly paid physical labour which only the lowest of the castes might perform, and for a white sahib—still more a mem-sahib—to do anything calling for physical exertion was most unseemly. No doubt there had been one or more powdered old sticks of fabulously wealthy widows watching from the luxurious villas on the shore and cursing the madcap girl and silly Norwegian for making fools of themselves and undermining the dirty natives' respect for decent people.

It did not matter to me what they thought, for I was leaving Srinagar the next day, and if I knew my oread, she would just dismiss such disapproval with a laugh.

What was my oread doing in that millionaire's paradise? I don't know the state of her bank account, but the reason for her being in Srinagar was that her father had a job in the military government there. What I do know is that she was young and fresh and darned attractive.

It was my oread who showed me Srinagar. For four days she and I did the rounds of polo grounds, swimming pools, houseboats and their wonderful gardens. We strolled in the streets with cars flashing past us and scattering donkeys, camels, cows and hens in all directions. On my last evening we went for a bicycle ride in the surrounding country and landed up at the ruins of a monastery, from where there was a magnificent view of the splendours of the Kashmir valley.

That old abode of monks was entirely overgrown with bushes and flowers. For quite a while we sat there chatting, then the pauses began to grow rather long and almost dangerous. A gossamer violet veil lay over Srinagar, Jhelum and Pir Panjal. Flocks of small birds settled in the pomegranate tree in front of us and spread like a colourful fan over its branches, and some grouse were cackling on the far side of some acacia bushes behind us.

I sat and thought of the days when I hung among filth and flies in Kuldsha and remembered my first faltering attempts to play Don Juan in Russian, Chinese and Turki

. . . There was a queer sensation in my throat and I wondered whether I should make a first try with a modest: 'I love you.'

To this day I can hear the ringing tones of my oread's laughter.

I don't know anything of the administration of Kashmir as it was then, but I imagine that with Captain Harrington Hawes in Kashmir Residency you were getting pretty near the top. Harrington Hawes and his gracious wife received me in such a way as to make me giddy, even after my experiences in Kashgar, Baltit and Gilgit.

They at once told me that I was to stay in Srinagar for several days, and from them I heard that there were weird rumours going around about the queer Norwegian who had come tramping across Mintaka all by himself. Harrington Hawes badly wanted to get me to a tailor to have a dinner jacket made, but fortunately I managed to avoid that. As a result there was an air of exclusivity about me in Srinagar society, for I was the only one among all those stiff shirts in the cool comfort of khaki.

In Kashmir Residency I lived like a prince. It was a big house and typically English, with many balconies, all sorts of additions and a confusion of windows. Perhaps it had a style, 'Tudor' or something else—I am not up in those things—but certainly it was a magnificent place and the garden with its flowerbeds and fountains under chinear trees was perhaps even more splendid.

One day Captain Harrington Hawes told me that he would like me to come to a cocktail party which a Dutch friend of his was giving. I was beginning to find it distasteful always appearing in khaki when others were dressed, and so I tried to get out of it. But there was no question of that, I was told: I was in a way the reason for the party and many of my host's friends had not yet met 'the Norwegian'. In the end I was fool enough to agree to borrow a dinner jacket from my host. He was a good bit taller than I, and when we drove off in the Captain's car I looked quite ridiculous.

The Dutchman's houseboat was a fairy-tale of luxury and was moored in one of the canals in the cool shade of some large trees. I did not feel at all right in my borrowed dinner jacket, and I was also a bit bothered by my bad English. Thus I don't think Mr Skrede made much of an impression when he was taken round and introduced to Lady This and Lady That, most of whom, by the way, were getting well on in years. But they were all very kind and pleasant. In fact they could not have been more interested if Mr Skrede had been a little Polar bear. They all said the same thing to comfort him:

'Don't you worry. We will win your country back for you, so that you can go back to your father and mother . . .'

All that 'don't you worry, my boy' began to get on my nerves, and I couldn't for the life of me see how old ladies sitting there drinking cocktails could have much say in the matter. But there were cocktails being handed round right and left and it was not long before I was talking English as well as any of them.

We Norwegians have a reputation in the great world for being rather inclined to boast and I am afraid I did nothing to make the Europeans in Srinagar think it anything but correct. You see, I told them that old Norway could manage very well by herself. Weren't Norwegian boats bringing their supplies across the Atlantic for them?

I hope I haven't given the reader a distorted picture

of the English in India. They were good enough. The younger men I saw were no doubt there because that was their place in the machinery of the mighty apparatus called the British Empire. None of them said a word about it. If they had been Norwegians, I should have had to listen to long tirades about how hellish it was being stuck there while others fought for home and country.

Otherwise they were like the usual run of Englishmen —not to be converted in their political opinions, superior and as self-assured as they could be, yet at the same time nice and helpful in every way, interested in travels and adventure, polite and correct to the nth degree. People of habit who poured cocktails down their throats at surprising speed and who would not have batted an eyelid if the wireless had suddenly announced the presence of a German Panzer Division at Rawalpindi, but who would have been horrified to find a double crease in their dinner jacket trousers.

You so often hear of the wicked English who subjugated poor India and sucked her dry. I don't know much about these things, but I very much wonder whether that view —taking it all in all—is not a pretty cheap one.

Since I was in Srinagar many things have happened. Not so very long ago we were able to read touching accounts of how India celebrated her freedom when the British departed and handed over the keys to the treasure-chests, of how maharajahs and dark-skinned industrial magnates leaped about in a state of exaltation together with beggars and the casteless, how hearts were bursting with happiness at their new-found freedom, of free distribution of meals and things, and of freedom medals for the poor— who in India are certainly not few.

I think I can see those processions, the well-fed maharajahs in gold-embroidered shirts and the poor with their free meals and freedom medals. The meals must have been popular all right, but what did the poor of India think when they were given a freedom medal to play with? It's a very great question whether they will ever achieve freedom from their own incredible sloth, if they will ever manage to summon up energy for anything but fanatical religious rioting and begging.

The dark-brown business gentry can now set about fleecing the people, and I imagine they know the art just as well as the British.

I was told that a white man could live in India for five rupees a day, provided he lived as simply as possible. The native workmen in the English and American factories seldom earned more than one or two rupees a day, and in many of the Indian factories they had to be content with five annas. Five annas a day? Men with families most of them—and in India a family usually means a fair number of mouths to feed. Is it any wonder there are Communists in India?

It is obvious that among three hundred and fifty million people there must be ten thousand who will do their utmost to make India a country in which everybody can live a human existence. It is very far from that yet, and one must hope that religion and politics won't cause too many murders.

While I have been sitting struggling with these chapters I have occasionally stopped to listen to the wireless. The announcer recently read out that religious rioting had cost the lives of forty-five thousand Mohammedans since India was liberated. God alone knows how many it will be before I have got the book finished.

I catch myself making comparisons:

I see the wonderful valley of Kashmir, as fertile and beautiful as a Garden of Eden; I see India's swarming masses demoralized to the bone by sloth and listlessness, disease, uncleanliness and religious fanaticism; I see the oases of Turkestan, where food grows by itself while people stand and watch it, and where filth and beastliness, laziness and superstition are boundless, and swarming humanity wary, deceitful, unreliable and incalculable. Then I find myself back again among the little dwelling places where the river Hunza winds along like a ribbon of silver threaded through the rugged hills. I see their tiny fields built on terraces of stone—so small that you could almost carry them in the hollow of your hand. There Mir Sahib's people go about light of foot like panthers, poor, but proud and self-assured, frank, honest and satisfied with the world and themselves.

The world is a queer place indeed!

Yet, perhaps I do know a pair of eyes that shone with joy on the day of India's freedom: the gentle and rather beautiful eyes of Mir Mohamed Nazim Khan. He who every day can look through his window at Rakapostu and Dhasto Ghil.

17. On Again

THE JOURNEY by car from Srinagar to Rawalpindi was so lovely that I just sat and wished it would never end. The road wound through a fine and fertile countryside, twisted through woods of cedar and chinear, straightened out across open pastures in which white hump-backed zebu cows grazed, cut across fields of rice and maize, and loitered through idyllic groves of oranges. The weather was perfect and no hotter than I would have wished.

We rushed past ox-carts on which sat peasants in white linen breeches with their hands under their chins meditating, past flocks of women carrying pots and baskets on their heads, and old women squatting outside reed huts and puffing at hookahs and looking into the distance.

Pir Panjal became remote and indistinct; the country grew flatter and flatter. We spent the night at a rest-house, and as we drew near to Rawalpindi the following afternoon, the temperature rose with every mile. By the time we reached the town it was so hot that the sweat had begun to trickle down us. We had only three or four hours in Rawalpindi. Round its railway station at least it is a fine town with broad streets, small pleasant restaurants and cosy gardens in front of most of the houses. Palms and banyans had now taken the place of poplars and willows.

The two days it took to reach Bombay by train passed like lightning. I was lucky to have the companionship of a Dane who had spent many years out East. He had been in Sinkiang, Mongolia, Siberia, Afghanistan, and he never ran out of stories about his travels. He had made a lot of money and had settled down in Srinagar to enjoy life.

Most of the passengers in our carriage were British or Indian soldiers. Some of the Indians were Gilgit Scouts; I knew them from the ibex head which some wore in their turbans, others on their garters.

At one station a well-dressed Indian came in and took a seat in our compartment. He took me for an Englishman and I did nothing to correct the impression. He was rather a chatterbox, and ended by putting me in a rather delicate position with his questions:

Was England fighting for the freedom of the nations?

She was indeed. And pretty stoutly too.

Well—perhaps then I could tell him why England didn't make India free?

That was a bit too stiff for me, and I could think of no other answer than that given me by an Englishman:

'Because they have to be here to keep you Hindus and Moslems from cutting each others' throats,' said I.

In Lahore and Delhi the stops were so short that I got no other impression than that of how miserably wretched was the position of the people. Outside the station townships lay unending monotonous plain lands, and the stop-

ping places with their clusters of poverty-stricken huts
and thin half-naked children were no elevating sight. For
the first few times it was rather fun watching the cackling,
yelling, squealing mass of bare arms and legs, black faces
and white breeches, baskets, packages and bundles hurl
itself at the train as it stopped, and how one and all clambered and trampled on each other to be first. But only the
first few times.

Then we were in Bombay, and that was a port and perhaps there would be a Norwegian boat there.

The fellow in the Norwegian consulate barely looked up
from his papers:

'No money today.'

'I asked to see the Consul. So far I haven't asked for
money.'

'Nothing today. Come some other time.'

'But . . .'

'You heard. There's none today.'

I know it's pretty hot in Bombay, but you don't travel
quite so far as I had, just to be told to come again some
other time. It wasn't many minutes before I was talking
with the Consul.

I learned that the others had gone to England only some
weeks previously, and I was also told that there was a
training camp for the Norwegian Navy at Bombay and
asked if I wouldn't like to join there. I said that I had no
objection to the Navy, only having set out to get to Little
Norway in Canada I would prefer to end up there if there
was any chance of getting a job on a boat going in that
direction. To my joy the Consul said he would help me.

You can't let an inquisitive young fellow loose in Bombay
for ten days without his seeing enough to make a chapter

in a book. But so many others have written about the white, black and yellow sides of Bombay that there seems little point in my adding to it. All I need say is that Consul Ahlsand helped me in every possible way, even to taking me with him and his wife for a day's sailing in their boat *Viking*. I paid a visit to the naval camp outside Colibar and there met a lad I had known in Stockholm. He told me he had met Andrew and Sverre and Atle in Cape Town, and that Kai, too, had been in Bombay and gone on to England.

One day I was told there was a boat for me, only it was in Karachi. Now I had a letter in my pocket, addressed to Captain Meling, s.s. *Ida Bakke* of Haugesand.

Captain Meling glanced up at me once or twice as he read the letter.

'I see. You want to go to New York?'

'Yes. But not for nothing.'

'Been at sea before?'

'No. But there's bound to be something I can do.'

'We'll see. Anyway, glad to have you aboard.'

I didn't get any wages or any work. Instead the Captain made me almost ashamed by putting me in the ship's best cabin, and I was fussed over as though I had been the owner's young daughter on a trip round the world.

By the time *Ida Bakke* left Karachi she had received new orders and made her way via Bombay to Singapore.

The British are fond of calling Singapore the Pearl of the Orient. It's true enough that when you come down the Malacca Straits on a day of bright sunshine, when the sea is like a mirror, and the palms on the low islands stand out sharply against the deep-blue sky, the approach is lovely. Even the aluminium coloured tanks fit in with the picture, the bungalows shine brightly among the greenery, and the whole looks clean and nice. The only possible objection is that the green is such a very greeny green that it almost hurts your eyes.

We had got pilot and doctor on board and were creeping slowly in through the narrow entrance. Some chalk-white little clouds were drifting peaceably across the sky, but on shore there were guns with muzzles pointing upwards, and the pilot had to be pretty cautious taking *Ida Bakke* through the mine field. Out in the harbour I could see the grim outlines of two British battleships.

By the time *Ida Bakke* had got herself settled by the quay all peace and beauty had vanished. There was nothing but dirty warehouses to be seen in all directions, and the quay swarmed with pitch black Malayan stevedores. We were to load rubber, and it was not long before the loading gang was hard at it. Their boss came aboard and sat directing the black devils who tore along with the bales of rubber as though the devil were at their heels. That boss was a greasy tough who had got himself a huge tropical helmet. In between the curses he kept flinging at the sweating half-naked Malays he spat blood in all directions. It looked horrible, but then I saw that, like all Malays, he was just chewing betel leaves, which makes spittle gory and no mistake.

I had palled up with a lad on board who came from Fredrikstad, and this Øyvind and I went for a tour as soon as we could get a pass ashore. As it happened we arrived in Singapore on my twentieth birthday, and as one is only twenty once in a lifetime and it isn't so often you go ashore in Singapore with a chap from Fredrikstad called Øyvind, it's obvious that the occasion was one which called for celebration.

We started off on the wrong foot, for the first place we got into was almost grisly with its cold marble walls and fresh flowers and fans puffing in your face. The public wasn't up to much either: ruminant Americans with a dollar atmosphere round them as thick as a Turkestan swarm of flies; Indians in turbans and Chinese in their finery; crafty little Japs who mustered us arrogantly through horn-rimmed spectacles; and British officers, as self-assured as ever, balancing their little canes between fore and middle fingers. Øyvind and I tucked ourselves away in a corner and made the smallest and cheapest drink we could get last as long as we could. Then, agreeing that the place did not suit our budget, we got out, turned the corner, popped into a den, and out again with a bottle of rum.

At our next port of call the waiter seemed a bit irritable when we ordered coca-cola, and if he thought we had a proper drink under the table, then he wasn't as stupid as he looked. Anyway, there we sat sipping rum and coca-cola and laying our plan of campaign for the evening. Who suggested a place where we could dance, I don't remember, nor who insisted that it must be a place with white girls, but we soon got ourselves going. We hailed a rickshaw. Øyvind was presumably the most experienced and better linguist, so he entered into negotiations with the yellow trotter in the shafts. He tried saying 'dance' and 'white girls' in all his languages, and I helped with mine, but the wretched Chinaman just looked blank. In pure desperation Øyvind rubbed his chin and shouted: 'White girls, like me!' and at that a look a comprehension appeared on the Chinaman's face.

We hopped into the rickshaw—chop-chop—and the Chink dashed off like a scared elk. We went up one street and down another and eventually came to a halt in front of a door ablaze with lights. The Chinaman got his money, and in we popped—straight into a barber's shop. That's what you get for rubbing your chin!

After that we reverted to Shank's pony and eventually found ourselves in the *New World*.

Some of the dance girls there were yellow and brown, but there were others who were white all right: fat Russians and small dark-haired dumpy Frenchwomen. The place was dominated by the British Navy: boys from the *Prince of Wales* and the glorious old *Repulse*, and they had taken over the dance floor, the bar, the Russians and every other girl irrespective of colour, build and nationality.

Øyvind and I managed to squeeze ourselves in at a table with some sailors. Perhaps I was a bit importunate in my desire to hear about the war:

'War? War's just——.' But they had had the luck of the devil. 'Sheer ruddy holiday being in Singapore keeping the Japs in check by just *showing* yourself.'

The following day we took things quietly. In the evening I paid a visit to a cinema, but was back early on board. I found the skipper in a deckchair on deck; the mate joined us, and then the chief engineer, and then a couple of chaps came across from another boat. The skipper fetched a bottle or two and we had a bit of a party. Apart from the drinks we were all Norwegian and, as such, never tired of talking of what had happened at home. So, when we had dealt with wind and weather, I had to tell them about April 9th in Oslo.

'I had been at the pictures—like this evening—went home early—like tonight—and just as I had got to sleep the air-raid alarm went. Like everybody else I thought it was a practise, but when the lights all went out, rumours started flying, and the telephones rang. In the morning it was all only too obvious—and it wasn't late in the day before the green devils were promenading up and down Karl Johan.'

The others sat there gazing into the distance over the harbour, their drinks forgotten, and saying 'Can you understand that such things happen?' Then I had to tell them what happened after that.

By the time I was down in my cabin pulling off my shirt, it must have been at least midnight. Just as I had got myself settled in my bunk, a boom sounded from the direction of the town. Just the one at first, then another, then several . . . Then silence for a few seconds, and after that the grisly sirens began wailing. The ack-ack guns started up, and with them came some dull bangs.

I dashed up on deck, Captain Meling was on the bridge calmly giving orders: 'Set look-outs fore and aft.'

We could see smoke and flames over the city. From up above, among the clouds, came the rising and falling drone of aeroplanes. It was not difficult to put two and two together.

The next day, it was December 8th, I saw that the battleships were gone from the harbour. I had to go up to the Immigration Department to see about certain formalities with my passport, and what a commotion there was! The police had been busy all night arresting every Jap in the place, and now they were being checked prior to being sent elsewhere. When I had had my passport stamped and got back into the street, the air-raid alarm went. The Japs were lined up against the walls, and the Australian soldiers straddled a bit lower behind their machine-guns. There was no superfluity of shelter space.

As for the visible results of the bombs, it seemed that one block of business buildings and the Chinese quarter had borne the brunt. It didn't amount, perhaps, to so very much as a bombing, but the really unpleasant thing was the heat which caused the smell of dead bodies to lie heavily over the city before they had time to clear them up.

The news was full of disasters: Pearl Harbour, then the *Prince of Wales* and *Repulse* were sunk.

For our last evening in Singapore Øyvind and I went back to *New World*. It was, perhaps, a little quieter there, but still bung full of sailors. Most of them were survivors from the two battleships, but don't imagine that made them more talkative. There was only one, and he had had a drop too much to drink, who kept snarling: 'We'll give them hell! We'll give them hell!'

It is a good many years since the war now, and the good and the evil are both being forgotten, which is perhaps no bad thing taking it all in all. Yet certain things stick. A landlubber who crosed the ocean in the heyday of the U-boat would be a bit peculiar in the top storey were he to forget it.

It was not that *Ida Bakke* was torpedoed, bombed or involved in anything dramatic on the voyage across the Indian Ocean and the South Atlantic to New York. It was perfectly peaceful. Nor shall I attempt to describe the atmosphere on board; that would be a bit beyond me. The lads just went about as though U-boats and devilry of that kind were just something they had heard about vaguely, and yet you knew perfectly well that they were on the alert every second of the day and night, that their nerves were attuned to the idea that the next moment they might be blown to smithereens, fried, roasted and slung far out into the sea.

There were plenty of tough jobs during the war, but those on shore and in the air were mostly made tolerable by pauses between the rounds. The sailors, however, were under strain almost uninterruptedly for those long years.

When Christmas Eve came *Ida Bakke* was off the south point of Madagascar. There were great preparations in the galley and elsewhere, but everyone told me that Christmas—pooh! that was an evening just like any other. They were so accustomed to spending Christmas at sea. For me, of course, it would be rather strange. First Christmas away from home, and in all that heat—and what with one thing and another.

The sun was right overhead, and the deck so hot that you could have fried an egg anywhere on it. Willy-nilly you began dreaming of snow-covered pines and gliding skis and home and Christmas fare; and thinking how father would have a drink because it was Christmas, and then a couple more because Christmas came only once a year. I was still pretty young, you see!

But it was Christmas all right. Christmas fare and no lack of Christmas drinks either. And carols, peace on earth and goodwill and all the rest of it. I don't think any clergyman has ever got me thinking about that as those weatherbitten seadogs did by singing the old carols: some pretty well in tune, others pretty well out of tune, and some of them already pretty red in the face. It seemed to occur to none of them that at that selfsame moment of peace and goodwill there might be a torpedo coming to rip up poor *Ida Bakke's* belly and distribute us between heaven and hell—in accordance with our deserts.

Other titles in the Equestrian Travel Classic series published by The Long Riders' Guild Press. We are constantly adding to our collection, so for an up-to-date list please visit our website: www.thelongridersguild.com

Title	Author
Southern Cross to Pole Star – Tschiffely's Ride	Aime Tschiffley
Tale of Two Horses	Aime Tschiffley
Bridle Paths	Aime Tschiffely
This Way Southward	Aime Tschiffely
Bohemia Junction	Aime Tschiffely
Through Persia on a Sidesaddle	Ella C. Sykes
Through Russia on a Mustang	Thomas Stevens
Across Patagonia	Lady Florence Dixie
A Ride to Khiva	Frederick Burnaby
Ocean to Ocean on Horseback	Williard Glazier
Rural Rides – Volume One	William Cobbett
Rural Rides – Volume Two	William Cobbett
Adventures in Mexico	George F. Ruxton
Travels with A Donkey in the Cevennes	Robert Louis Stevenson
Winter Sketches from the Saddle	John Codman
Following the Frontier	Roger Pocock
On Horseback in Virginia	Charles Dudley Warner
California Coast Trails	J. Smeaton Chase
My Kingdom for a Horse	Margaret Leigh
The Journeys of Celia Fiennes	Celia Fiennes
On Horseback through Asia Minor	Fred Burnaby
The Abode of Snow	Andrew Wilson
A Lady's Life in the Rocky Mountains	Isabella Bird
Travels in Afghanistan	Ernest F. Fox
Through Mexico on Horseback	Joseph Carl Goodwin
Caucasian Journey	Negley Farson
Turkestan Solo	Ella K. Maillart
Through the Highlands of Shropshire	Magdalene M. Weale
Wartime Ride	J. W. Day
Across the Roof of the World	Wilfred Skrede
Woman on a Horse	Ana Beker
Saddles East	John W. Beard
Last of the Saddle Tramps	Messanie Wilkins
Ride a White Horse	William Holt
Manual of Pack Transportation	H. W. Daly
Horses, Saddles and Bridles	W. H. Carter
Notes on Elementary Equitation	Carleton S. Cooke
Cavalry Drill Regulations	United States Army
Horse Packing	Charles Johnson Post
14th Century Arabic Riding Manual	Muhammad al-Aqsarai
The Art of Travel	Francis Galton
Shanghai à Moscou	Madame de Bourboulon
Saddlebags for Suitcases	Mary Bosanquet
The Road to the Grey Pamir	Ana Louise Strong
Boot and Saddle in Africa	Thomas Lambie
To the Foot of the Rainbow	Clyde Kluckhohn
Through Five Republics on Horseback	George Ray
Journey from the Arctic	Donald Brown
Saddle and Canoe	Theodore Winthrop
The Prairie Traveler	Randolph Marcy
Reiter, Pferd und Fahrer – Volume One	Dr. C. Geuer
Reiter, Pferd und Fahrer – Volume Two	Dr. C. Geuer

The Long Riders' Guild
The world's leading source of information regarding equestrian exploration!
www.thelongridersguild.com

www.ingramcontent.com/pod-product-compliance
Lightning Source LLC
Chambersburg PA
CBHW020609270326
41927CB00005B/245